KEW PAST

David Blomfield

Phillimore

1994

Published by
PHILLIMORE & CO. LTD.
Shopwyke Manor Barn, Chichester, Sussex

ISBN 0 85033 923 5

Printed and bound in Great Britain by
BIDDLES LTD.
Guildford, Surrey

KEW PAST

Print of St Anne's, 1851.

Contents

Acknowledgements

The author and publisher are indebted to the following galleries, collections and individuals who have kindly provided illustrations and/or given permission for their use: The London Borough of Richmond upon Thames, Local Studies Collection, Jacket, Frontispiece, 4, 5, 6, 9, 16, 21, 23, 25, 27, 34, 37, 38, 41, 45, 50, 53, 56, 57, 60, 64, 65, 74, 89, 95, 96, 105, 107, 113, 116, 117, 122, 130, 136, 143, 151, 152, 155, 156, 166, 168; The London Borough of Richmond upon Thames, Orleans House Collection (Photographs by John King), 32, 44, 58, 63, 67; Julian Wolfreys, 8, 17, 18, 20, 24, 30, 47, 59, 62, 66, 80, 81, 82, 87, 99, 102, 109, 133, 159, 160, 169; The Queen's School, Kew, 13, 23, 29, 35, 61, 73, 78, 79, 120, 121; The Royal Botanic Gardens, Kew, 39, 54, 76, 88, 97, 112, 125, 131; Courtaulds PLC, 107; Jim Keesing, 55, 115, 124. 129, 134, 135, 140, 144, 165, 167; The Public Record Office, 43; The Museum of Richmond, 156; The Museum of London, 2; The London Borough of Hounslow, 28, 31, 71; Maisie Brown, 84; Raymond Gill, 86; Barbara and Adrian Rundle, 161; Elizabeth Lloyd, 133; John Cloake, 12; Kathleen Cassidy, 164; Vivian Erlebach, 93; Iris Bolton, 94; Henry Engleheart, 68, 90-2; *The Greyhound*, Kew Green, 118; The Duke of Northumberland (Photographs by English Life Publications), 7, 10, 26; By courtesy of the National Portrait Gallery, London, 22, 46; Reproduced by permission of the Trustees of the Wallace Collection: 48, 69; The Harris Museum and Art Gallery, 111; The National Maritime Museum, 33; The Royal Collection © 1994, Her Majesty the Queen, 14, 36; Tate Gallery, London, 110; St Paul's Church, Brentford (Photograph by Patrick White), 49; St Anne's Church, Kew (Photography by R.J.L. Smith of Much Wenlock); 100, 101, 103, 106; Peter Chaplin, 119; Ann Bissell Thomas, 70; Michael and Frances Atwood, 72, 85; Darell School, Kew, 137; Peter and John Newens, 108, 153; Robert Smith, 51, 52, 75, 127; Pamela Ryan, 138, 139; David Matten, 163; J.Hickey Ltd.,154; Ann Abercrombie, 162.

Introduction

Kew has an ancient name, Saxon in origin. Its history, however, is more ancient still, as for centuries it marked the lowest point at which the Thames could be regularly crossed on foot. This ford, and the ferry that succeeded it, gave Kew its original name of Cayho or Cyho—a quay (Cay) on a spur of land (ho). There were 22 other variants before it generally settled down to Kew in the 17th century, as spelling was a very variable business until then. The reader of this book will, for example, find several disconcerting variations in the way families spelt their own names.

That original 'spur' must have referred to no more than a small patch of land around the southern end of the ford, but for the 10,000 who now live in Kew, and for the millions who visit the Gardens, the derivation of the name seems peculiarly appropriate. The Kew of today certainly covers a spur of land—a considerable peninsula formed by the Thames—and a quay is still there, though not exactly where it used to be.

Our 20th-century Kew is in fact made up of three areas. These are now almost indistinguishable from one another, but each has its own distinct history. The first area—that around the Green—traces its origins back to the days of the first quay. The second, which includes much of the Botanic Gardens and most of the land between the railway and the Gardens wall, was treated as part of Richmond until the 1890s. The third area, which is now bounded by the railway and the A316, only became part of Kew in this century; before that it was linked to Mortlake, though it boasted a medieval manor of its own.

This book covers the story of all three areas, tracing so far as possible their growth from prehistoric and medieval communities to the modern Kew. Most of the story is taken from documentary and oral evidence, but some inevitably involves legend and rumour that cannot now be proved or disproved. Where there is substantial doubt or lack of proof for any statement, the reader will find the uncertainty signalled by the use of phrases such as 'maybe' or 'it is said that'. Where there are no such signposts, the author is implying that he has substantial evidence, and is prepared to defend his case!

The majority of the illustrations come either from the archives of Richmond's excellent Local History Library, or from photographs taken specifically for the book. For the former I am especially grateful to Jane Baxter, and for the latter to Julian Wolfreys and John King. As this book is being published exactly one hundred years after the creation of the first British postcards, several of these have been used as illustrations, most of them contributed by Jim Keesing from his own comprehensive collection of Kew postcards.

Although the author is solely responsible for what is included in the text, he is hugely indebted to many friends in Kew and especially to his fellow local historians for their generous help. Some, like George Cassidy, left their invaluable work behind them for their successors to build on. Others, such as John Cloake, Iris Bolton, Gillian Clegg, Christopher May, George Speight, and Raymond Gill, are regular and expert contributors to the local history archives of Richmond and Mortlake. Without their patient help this book could never have been attempted.

Prehistoric Kew

The ford at Kew, around which the first of its huts must have clustered, lay some two hundred yards up river from the Brentford Ferry Gate of Kew Gardens. It was very probably used from prehistoric times. Certainly a number of iron-age and bronze-age artefacts have been found all along the Surrey and Middlesex banks on either side of the ford. Most of these are weapons: any advantage the ford may have offered in the way of trade would have been considerably offset by the inconvenience of being periodically devastated by passing armies.

However, these are not the oldest remains. Although it seems likely that the Thames valley was first occupied by humans about 440,000 years ago, animals may well have been there far earlier. The remains of mammoth, hippopotamus, hyena, bison and elephant have been found on either bank, while Kew has one record to itself: during the building of its railway line, workers unearthed the only bone of a polar bear ever found in the London area.

Other construction work has unearthed equally unexpected finds. A human skull of about 500 B.C. was dug up during work on a drainage scheme a little upriver from the ford, and slender flint axes of that period, known as Thames picks, have been found all along the stretch from Syon to Kew Bridge. In the 1930s an early Bronze Age beaker was turned up by workmen laying down a tennis court in West Hall Road.

There are undoubtedly more finds to come. One of the oldest prehistoric implements unearthed around Kew, a flint axe head, was found off Stanmore Road, well away from the river, and as recently as 1993. It seems likely that it could have been disturbed initially by a wartime bomb. If that is so, there could well be many more such finds yet to be made by other sharp-eyed gardeners.

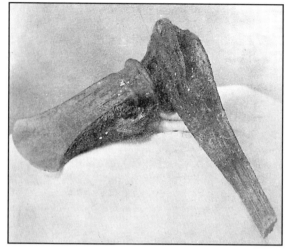

1 A bronze celt (axe), recovered from the Thames during the building of the third Kew Bridge in 1903 (see page 109).

2 Iron-age tankard. Found in the Thames between Brentford and Kew, this bronze cup holds about four pints, and was probably used for communal imbibing at feasts.

The Warlords

Written history for Kew begins in 54 B.C. with Julius Caesar's *Gallic Wars*. In his account of his second punitive raid on Britain, Caesar described in some detail his route from the Kent coast to Cassivellaunus' stronghold north of the Thames. He learned that the river was fordable 'at one place only', about seventy-five miles from the sea. When he reached the ford, he found the Britons opposing his crossing, and the bank 'fenced by large stakes fixed along the edge'. The two most likely sites for this crossing are Coway, near Walton, and Kew. Stakes have been discovered at Coway, and on both sides of the ford between Kew and Brentford, where the line of stakes stretched all the way from Isleworth to Kew Bridge. Historians are split on the issue, but as Kew was on the shorter route to

the British camp, which was near St Albans, it has logically the better claim.

The next recorded mention of the ford is in the Anglo-Saxon Chronicle. In 1016 the Danes under Canute and the Saxons under Edmund Ironside fought a series of battles on both sides of the ford. The fighting proved futile. The Saxons, as was so often the case, won the battles, only to lose the war: before the year was out, Edmund was dead and the field left clear for Canute. For Kew too nothing changed. If one of the battles was fought, as seems likely, right across what is now the Royal Botanic Gardens, the contestants—or more likely the camp followers—did an excellent job in tidying up after the event. No signs of the fighting remain.

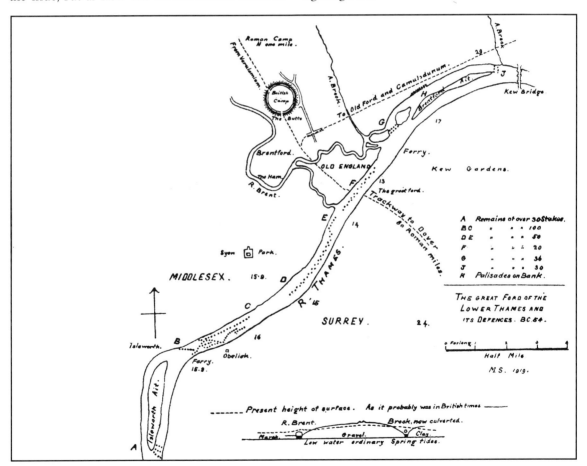

3 The Great Ford and its defences in 54 B.C.—as mapped by the antiquarian Montagu Sharpe—indicating the sites of the stakes removed from the Thames in the 19th century.

Royal Relations

Kew is not named for certain in any record before 1314. Then it is mentioned five times—in the Survey of the Manor of Shene. It could not have made a more a modest entrance, or a more appropriate one, as those five mentions are of villeins (serfs) working for the Lord of the Manor.

'Gilbert of Cyho' seems to have been typical. He held 18 acres of farming land and two acres of meadow. Each year he had a set commitment to his lord: three shillings; two quarters of malt for brewing ale; 10 eggs at Easter; seven days ploughing; half a day's sowing; work at haymaking time until finished—providing two men for the harvest every other day; two days carting corn; one hurdle for the sheep-fold; folding fleeces at sheep shearing. In return, the lord provided food for his tenants while they worked for him—a halfpenny loaf and a farthing's worth of fish, fish being the staple diet of riverside communities.

4 Charles Brandon, Duke of Suffolk. Three of Suffolk's letters appear in the State Papers, addressed in turn, with ducal disregard for consistency, from Kaio, Kaw, and Kayhoo.

5   Charles Somerset, Earl of Worcester.

This was a significant century for such villeins, as in 1358 Edward III turned Shene Manor into a palace, and began what would be a long love affair between a whole succession of kings and this stretch of the Thames. Attracted partly by hunting, and partly by a desire to escape as far as possible from the stench and disease of London, the kings built and rebuilt this palace over the next hundred years, to the benefit of local trade. Henry V, now remembered mostly for his success in war, built two religious houses close by, to expiate his father's sin in robbing Richard II of his throne and life. The first was a Carthusian monastery, built to the south west of where Kew Observatory now stands, and the second a convent at Syon. Kew's ford lay between the two. It became a ferry and flourished, so much so that 'Kayo' was rated taxable in 1483.

The tax was minimal, but it was a sign that Kayo was already a substantial hamlet.

Throughout those dying days of the feudal system, Kew's modest fortunes must have depended almost entirely on the ferry, its buildings clustering around the landing stage. With the arrival of the Tudors, however, everything changed. For in the next century, if Kew never quite grasped power itself, at least it was touched by its fringes.

Henry VII's government was radically centralised on his own palaces, and the palace he favoured was Shene. It was again rebuilt, and renamed after his Yorkshire earldom of Richmond. No longer able to disregard the King, the barons saw that, if they wanted influence, they had to dance attendance at the palace; so they looked for estates at a convenient distance from Richmond; and nothing was more convenient than Kew.

The first to settle there were Henry's relations, the Earl of Devon and Charles Somerset. The Earls of Devon bought land along the riverside, upstream of the ferry. Charles Somerset, Earl of Worcester, settled to the east of them in Kew Park. Thomas Byrkis, a less powerful but apparently wealthy gentleman, occupied a big house by the ferry, which would be known as Kew Farm.

With the accession of Henry VIII, Kew gained further glamour. We know from his accounts that he disembarked from his barge at Kew on his way from the city to Richmond, presumably to cut across the peninsula on horseback. It is probable that he left the barge at the dock which then led into Kew pond. In view of this, not surprisingly two of his closest friends decided to buy homes next to his route. Kew Farm went to Henry Norris, and a new house, built by Somerset a little to the east of Kew Farm, went to the grandest of all the Tudor grandees, the Duke of Suffolk.

Suffolk had married Henry VIII's sister Mary, who had briefly been Queen of France, and determinedly retained the title for the rest of her life. A chronicler of the time wrote that Kew was famed as an elegant village, but added diplomatically that it was still more famous for her presence there.

Royal Revenge

Life for the nobility under the Tudors was always a bit of a lottery. It might be glamorous, but it tended to be short—and the closer you were to the sovereign, the greater the chance of decapitation. Everything turned either on the whim of the King, or of his Lord Chancellor, especially if it concerned the succession to the throne. In Kew, although we cannot always know exactly who owned what, we can see that properties changed hands with extraordinary speed.

The first to go was Henry Norris. 'Esquire of the Body' to the King, he was executed, ironically, for adultery with the body of the Queen, Anne Boleyn. His house, Kew Farm, might now have reverted to its former comfortable obscurity, but instead it began to move even further into the centre of Tudor politics. First, it was granted to the new Queen's brother, Edward Seymour, who as Duke of Somerset would later become Protector to his nephew Edward VI. He rejected it, however,

6 Edward Courtenay, Earl of Devon. One of a much-executed Catholic family, Edward was a popular candidate for marriage to Mary I. In their youth both lived in Kew.

and it was sold to John Dudley, who as Duke of Northumberland would also become Protector of Edward VI, but not before executing his predecessor.

Next to fall was Henry Courtenay, Earl of Devon. Descended from Edward IV, he was obviously suspect. He was influential too: the earliest record we have of the tolls of Kew ferry is a bill for taking six of his horses across when he was entertaining the Duke of Burgundy. He was also wealthy. The State Papers of the time, which are uncannily like the secret papers of Hoover's FBI, show that the Lord Chancellor, Thomas Cromwell, had been carefully assessing the value of his estates.

The Courtenays had always found life at Kew precarious. Henry Courtenay's father had been temporarily evicted at the end of Henry VII's reign, and for a time the King apparently lodged Catherine of Aragon in his house while she was, as it were, between princes—Prince Arthur had died and the King was trying to squeeze an increase in dowry before marrying her to the future Henry VIII. It must have been a humiliating experience for Catherine, but with typical lack of sensitivity Henry many years later sent her daughter Mary also to a house in Kew. She seems to have stayed for scarcely two years. The atmosphere was hardly congenial.

For the ordinary folk in Kew, things were not much better. They too were suffering from the whims of the King. Their lives, probably just as short as those of the nobility and considerably more nasty and brutish, still revolved around the ferry. On their first appearance in Tudor records, they seem to be have been typical Kewites—they are battling for their rights. The King had granted a monopoly on the ferry—on which the charge was one halfpenny for every man and horse, and one farthing for every man, woman and child. They were complaining that the ferryman was charging a levy on any local boatman who took passengers across the river in his own boat. Unfair, said the local boatmen. Maybe it was, but they got no recompense.

The result of their petition was of course not so surprising, but the monopoly was an oddity in itself. It had been granted to John Hale, 'servant of

The Tudor Relatives at Kew

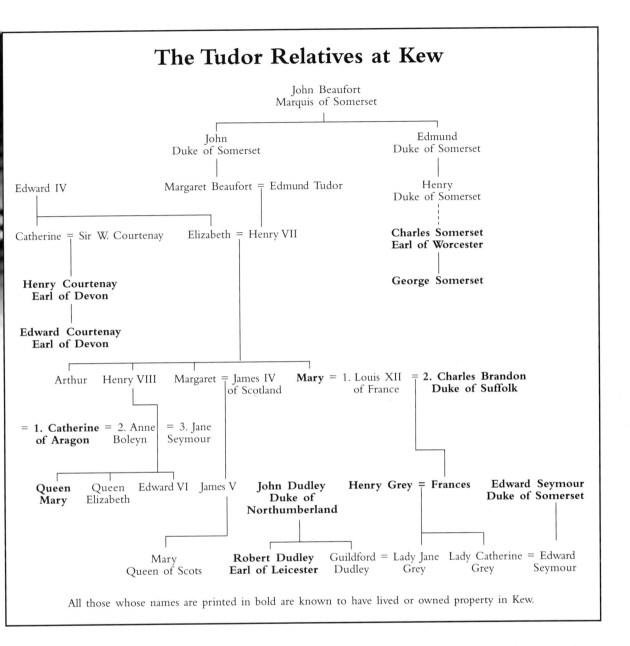

All those whose names are printed in bold are known to have lived or owned property in Kew.

Henry Norris'—typical, it might seem, of a courtier pulling strings for his servant. (Even Suffolk was not too proud to solicit favours for his servants from the all-powerful Thomas Cromwell.) Not so! The monopoly was granted six months *after* Norris had been executed for treason. It seems that Hale could have sold his master for the small change of Kew ferry.

The Fishermen of Kew

The ferry may have been the first excuse for litigation in Kew, but over the next three centuries it would never match fishing as the major source of friction. This was understandable, as fishing was Kew's and Brentford's largest industry.

There are still echoes of that industry in the name Westerly Ware, which until the 18th century stretched from the dock as far as Ferry Lane. Almost certainly this was one of two areas in Kew where the fishermen beached their boats, and dried

7 Edward Seymour, Duke of Somerset.

8 Kew Pond. Perhaps once a medieval fish pond and then a dock for the royal barge, the pond later became the Victorian equivalent of a car wash, the ramp in the foreground being used by carters for watering their horses, cleaning their carts and soaking the wooden wheels when the iron rims worked loose.

and mended their nets. The other area was further downstream beyond the dock, marked as the Ware Ground, which presumably was originally the 'Easterly Ware'. Both would have been named after the 'weirs' the fishermen set up across the river. These weirs were made generally of hurdles set zig-zag fashion, in which the fish would be caught, then collected in nets and dragged to shore. In those days there was no towpath, and only narrow channels were left for the boats. Consequently quarrels between fishermen and boatmen were inevitable, as each accused the other of restraint of trade.

The fishermen worked mostly for those who held specific rights to certain stretches of the river. In Kew these included for many years the Carthusian monastery of Shene, which almost certainly had rights along Westerly Ware, and Merton Priory which owned the Ware Ground. The Winchester diocese also had a fish pond at Kew at one time—perhaps it was Kew pond before it housed the royal barge.

In the 16th century Holinshed says that no river in Europe had more salmon than the Thames, in addition to 'Barbels, Trouts, Pearches, Smelts,

Breames, Roches, Daces, Gudgings, Flounders, Shrimps'. For any failings he blamed the 'avarice of fishermen'. Even in the days of Edward III there had been petitions to restrict the number of weirs, and nets below a certain width of mesh. It was ever so. The Thames may now have lost its fish, but little else has changed. The arguments today in Brussels on over-fishing are very similar.

Fishing rights were prized and profitable, and there were inevitably quarrels between the owners of the weirs, especially as sovereigns tended to grant new rights with a royal disregard for previous grants, and indeed for whether the rights were theirs to grant, or belonged as many did to the City of London. In 1549 Kew fishermen petitioned the Court of Aldermen to remove a weir recently set up by the Duke of Somerset—presumably off the Syon bank. They were recommended to make humble suit to his Grace, and 'in case they were not holpen thereby that they shulde repayer hither agin for their further aid'. Meanwhile, they were assured, his Grace would be reminded of the statutes against his encroachment. There is no record of whether this brave protest succeeded.

The Kingmakers

The fishermen's protest was particularly remarkable because at that time Somerset was the most powerful man in England. When, years before, he had declined the house in Kew, and allowed it to be sold to the ambitious but less well connected John Dudley, it must have seemed a slight on Kew, especially as Somerset went on to establish far greater estates on the former, now dissolved, religious houses next door at Syon and Richmond. Then on Henry's death in 1546 he became Protector to his young nephew Edward VI. How then did the fishermen of Kew even dare to question his right to put a weir wherever he might please?

The answer may well lie in the date they chose to act. It was in 1549, and 1549 was not a good year for Somerset. First he was forced to sign his own brother's death warrant for treason; then he failed to cope with a comparatively minor uprising led by Robert Kett. Even worse, the uprising was put down by his rival John Dudley, the same John Dudley who had bought the house in Kew. Dudley was now plotting to succeed Somerset, and no doubt encouraged anyone however humble—even local fishermen—that might be ready to embarrass him.

By the end of 1549 Somerset had fallen, and Dudley (created Duke of Northumberland) succeeded both to his rôle as Lord Protector, and to his estates in Syon and Richmond. Kew now was at the very hub of Tudor politics, not just because of Northumberland's Kew estate but—still more crucially—because of the Suffolks' house. It had been inherited by their son in law, Henry Grey, whose daughter, the Lady Jane Grey, was a likely claimant to the throne if Edward VI were to die.

Hastily Lady Jane was married to Northumberland's son. Richmond, Syon and Kew were now linked not only by marriage, but by a shared ambition: that, on Edward's imminently expected death, the crown would pass to Lady Jane Grey, and—more importantly—the power would remain with Northumberland.

The natural heir was Princess Mary, also formerly of Kew. Mary, however, was a Catholic, and Northumberland calculated that she would have little popular support. His calculations however were awry, and his mistake would cost the Greys and Northumberlands their lives.

9 John Dudley, Duke of Northumberland.

10 Lady Jane Grey. Very probably, as a child, Lady Jane stayed at Kew: her grandparents and parents had estates there.

The First Kew Gardener

The clash between the Kingmakers—Somerset and Northumberland—not only embroiled the great lords of Kew, most of whom lost their heads over the issue, and some of its poorest fishermen, who presumably lost, and never recovered, much of their profits to those Syon weirs; it also caught up another inhabitant of Kew, William Turner, who came from a significant new class, part academic, part clerical, which was gradually making its influence felt in England for the very first time.

11 The page from Turner's *Herbal* where the Father of English Botany says of the chick pea, 'I have it in my garden at Kew'.

Turner was born poor—he was possibly the son of a tanner—but was brilliant enough to attract patronage and gain a fellowship at Pembroke Hall in Cambridge. He specialised in medicine and botany. He was also a committed follower of the new religion—one of a group of young men who spearheaded the Reformation in England, two of whom, Latimer and Ridley, were to earn their own Martyrs Memorial in Oxford. Ridley taught Turner Greek.

The Duke of Somerset, equally committed to the reformed religion, employed Turner as his doctor at Syon. Turner took a house in Kew, where he cultivated a garden and, being more interested in botany than medicine, he resented the time he had to spend in Syon. In three years and a half, he wrote, he had no more than three weeks 'to bestowe upon ye seekyng of herbes, and markyng in what places they grow'.

References in his *Herbal*, the first edition of which was published in 1551, indicate that he grew exotic plants in this garden. We do not know where the garden was, but it is peculiarly appropriate that the man now known as the Father of English Botany should have practised it personally at Kew, though more than two centuries before the Botanic Gardens were established there.

With the rapid switches of power, first from Somerset to Northumberland, then to the Catholic Queen Mary, and then back again to the Protestant Queen Elizabeth, life for Turner could not have been easy. In the State Papers of 1549 there is a reference to the 'embezzling of goods of the late Lord Protector by his servants'. 'Certain stuff,' it says, 'was conveyed by boats by night to Kew ... The Duke had three servants living in the town, Sir Myles Partridge, Turner his physician, and Gely, gentleman usher.'

We do not know the outcome, but this reference raises two interesting points. First, 'embezzlement' of this kind seems to have been excusable: it was certainly excused, as within a year Turner was Dean of Wells, and after a necessary flight abroad in Mary's reign he returned to publish subsequent editions of his *Herbal*. Secondly, it seems that Kew, though scarcely a hamlet, was then of sufficient importance to be described for the first and last time ever as a town.

Elizabethan Revels

The swing of the pendulum, first to the Catholic Mary and then to the Protestant Elizabeth, inevitably led to yet more changes in Kew. Briefly the Catholic Courtenays were restored to their estates upriver, but only for Elizabeth to throw them out and give her favourite Robert Dudley, Earl of Leicester, both their lands and those of his father, Northumberland. So Leicester now owned Kew Farm, the Devon lands and the house once occupied by the Suffolks and later by the Greys.

Kew Park, the other big estate in Kew, had changed hands too, also going to a favourite of the Queen, though a man of a very different stamp. Its new owner was Dr. Awberry, a distinguished lawyer who was one of the delegates for the trial of Mary, Queen of Scots, and was 'a great stickler for the saving of her life'. Despite—or it could have been because of—this, Queen Elizabeth had a great affection for her 'little doctor', as she called him. The Doctor's grandson, John Aubrey, tells us in his book *Brief Lives* that Awberry was a close friend of the astrologer Dr. Dee, who lived 'at Mortlake, not a mile distant'.

We do not know if Elizabeth visited Awberry, but she certainly visited Kew. It is said that when she stayed at Richmond Palace she would ride across to meet Leicester beneath an elm on the riverside. It grew on what was for centuries called Queen Elizabeth's Lawn. Sadly though, all that remains for us to see is a stretch of tarmac—the Lawn is now the Gardens riverside car park—and a kitchen table in Queen Victoria's Osborne House in the Isle of Wight, which was made from the elm when it fell in a storm in the 19th century.

The romantic Leicester fell too. Suspected of killing his first wife, Amy Robsart, in 1560, he was ordered by Elizabeth to stay in Kew until the scandal blew over. Yet, the scandal persisted, and

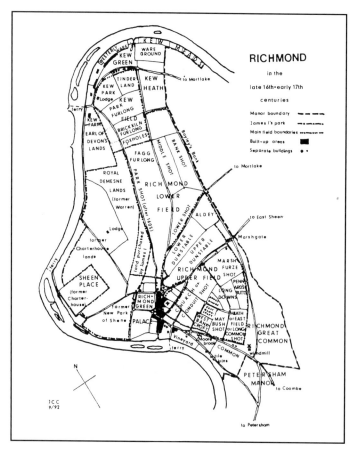

12 The Manor of Richmond. This map, the work of John Cloake, illustrates where the big houses of Kew stood at the end of the 16th century. The Lodge in Kew Park was later extended and rebuilt to become the first Kew Palace.

any hopes that Leicester may have entertained of marriage to the Queen proved vain. His influence declined and, perhaps because Elizabeth no longer visited him beneath the elm, he sold his Kew estates.

Briefly they went to Thomas Gardiner, a teller of the Exchequer, but Gardiner was caught with his hand in the Treasury and had to sell. They were then bought by a gentleman called Hugh Portman, who was subsequently knighted by Elizabeth herself on a visit to Kew. To have extracted a knighthood from Elizabeth, Portman must have been a man of considerable means. We have a record of how much it cost Portman's relative, Sir John Puckering, simply to give her Majesty a dinner.

Puckering also lived at Kew, very probably renting a house—perhaps the old Kew Farm—from Portman. At the time he was the Lord Keeper of the Great Seal and Speaker of the House of Commons. A contemporary recorded the visit from the arrival of the great queen at her humble subject's gate. It all went as expected.

At her first alighting she had a fine fan, with a handle garnished with diamonds. When she was in the middle way, between the garden gate and the house, there came one running towards her with a nosegay in his hands and delivered it with a short, well-penned speech; it had in it a very rich jewel, with many pendants of diamonds, valued at £400 at least. After dinner, in her privy chamber he presented her with a fine gown and juppin, which things were pleasing to Her Highness, and to grace his lordship the more, she of herself took from him a salt, a spoon, and a fork of fine agate.

Few tears should be shed for Sir John's lost cutlery. He knew exactly what he was about. Every bit as mean as Elizabeth, he was also corrupt. Both sovereign and subject knew to the last spoon how much his supper was worth.

13 Queen Elizabeth's Elm.

14 Robert Dudley, Earl of Leicester. This portrait (in the Queen's Hampton Court collection, but not on display) is one of a number of pictures bought by the Capel family, who in the following century settled next door to Leicester's Kew estate.

Stuart Siblings

In 1603 Elizabeth died, after spending days trying to fend off fate by remaining on her feet. Appropriately she chose Richmond Palace for this final dramatic performance, for she was to be the last of a long line of sovereigns for whom it was a favoured home. Her successors, the Stuart kings, preferred to live elsewhere.

Yet there was one last flurry of activity there that would once again involve Kew. James I might disregard Richmond, but his eldest son Henry loved it. This young Prince of Wales, who was to die too soon to lose his reputation for being perhaps the most gifted heir ever to the British throne, set up his own Camelot court in Richmond. Here he collected pictures, horses, and a coterie of talented friends.

One close companion, the poet and sailor Arthur Gorges, settled nearby in Kew Park. Prince Henry's sister, Elizabeth Stuart, famous for her beauty and charm, stayed at the old Kew Farm theoretically under the care of Lord John Harington. From a letter he wrote in 1609, preserved in the State Papers, we can gather that Harington's job was far from easy: 'Oct 25 from Kew John Lord Harrington to Salisbury. Cannot wait in person with the book of accounts for the Princess Elizabeth; the Prince often calling for her to ride with him necessitates his own constant attendance.'

Also in attendance much of the time were two especially close friends of the Prince: Harington's son John and Robert Carr, Earl of Ancrum. The former probably stayed in Kew Farm with his father, but the latter settled permanently in Kew, buying up much of the Portman property.

However, the days of riding and romancing in Richmond were to be short. Henry died in 1612, to be succeeded as heir by a brother who shared his taste for art but would lose his head over other more practical matters of state. Then Elizabeth left Kew to marry a minor German princeling and achieve fame for the brevity of their rule as the Winter King and Queen of Bohemia. In exile Elizabeth raised a large family, one of whom, Rupert of the Rhine, proved a dashing if undisciplined cavalry commander for his uncle in the Civil War. It was, however, Elizabeth's youngest child, Sophia, who ironically proved to be the most influential. She married the Elector of Hanover, and by a strange twist of fate her descendants not only found themselves kings of England, but would choose to settle on the estates where Elizabeth Stuart and her brother used to ride more than a century before.

15 Henry Stuart, Prince of Wales, with John Lord Harington. By an unknown British painter, this is the only surviving joint picture of these close friends.

16 *(facing page)* Elizabeth Stuart—an 18th-century engraving of a contemporary portrait. The family tree illustrates the link between the Stuart and Hanoverian royal families; both had homes in Kew.

ELISABETH PR. PAL.
QVEEN of BOHEMIA.

From an Original painted by Ger.d Honthorst   in the Royal appartments at S.t James's.

G. Vertue del. & Sculp.

15

The Dutch House

With the departure of the Stuart siblings, Kew settled into a more sober, gentlemanly, phase. It still had its big houses, but they now came into the hands of those who cared more for the estates themselves than for their convenient location. Though little more than a hamlet, it began to acquire something of the shape of a traditional English village.

Tudor Kew had had a village green, but of unusual shape. It was far longer then than it is today, as it stretched all the way from the pond to the ferry, narrowing as it passed Kew Park. There had however been hardly any houses for the villagers round the Green. Most of them must have lived along the river bank or around the mansions where they were employed. However, in the last years of Elizabeth, and increasingly under the Stuarts, Kew Green was gradually narrowed as the Richmond Manor granted plots on its fringes with permission to build. In nearly every case only cottages were built initially, but in time all of them would be replaced by the more substantial houses we see today.

The residue of Sir Hugh Portman's estate was handed down his line of sons, until the youngest sold it outright. Part of it, including Portman's own house, which was possibly on the site of the Suffolks' mansion, had by then been let to a merchant called Samuel Fortrey. Now Fortrey bought the house, and in 1631 he decided to rebuild it.

With that decision we move from sparse written records on to the bricks and mortar that we can recognise and enjoy today; for what Fortrey built was the Dutch House. It is now generally known as Kew Palace, but the old name is still sometimes used, if only because of its distinctive style of architecture. It was built in the Netherlandish style, which was fashionable at the time. Perhaps it had a special appeal for Fortrey, who was Flemish by birth, though entirely British by upbringing. He was in fact the quintessential immigrant, having been born in the middle of the English Channel on a boat in which his parents were fleeing from the Spanish Inquisition. He married another Lowlander, Catherine La Fleur of Hainault. The house has been altered in minor details since they built it, but we can still see their initials and the date of the building intertwined above the front doorway.

What we cannot see, but are still there beneath the ground floor, are the remains of an older building. This undercroft is presumably all that is left of Portman's house, or possibly of the Suffolks' which preceded it. The Dutch House is therefore not only the oldest house in Kew, but probably inherits at least the foundations of one of the great Tudor mansions.

There are no prints of the house from the 17th century, but it seems clear that there were meadows rather than gardens then between the house and the river. There is a record that in addition to 'Barns,

17   The Fortrey initials on the Dutch House.

18 The Dutch House today—almost unaltered from the original.

Stables, Edifices', Fortrey's seven acres included 'Woods, Underwoods, Orchards and Gardens'— very probably stretching along towards today's Herbarium.

Two other big houses were also changing hands at this time. Kew Farm was apparently acquired by the Earl of Ancrum, who rebuilt the old house on an even greater scale. Meanwhile the lodge in Kew Park (later to be known as Kew House) was sold by Gorges' heir to Sir Richard Bennett, son of the Sheriff of London. Bennett was a merchant, but his chief interests seem to have centred on extending his estate by buying up what he could from Ancrum.

This gentlemanly pursuit of building up estates in Kew was now rudely interrupted by the Civil War. Kew itself was not directly affected, though Brentford was the site of one of the fiercer battles. One of the aits (islands) however is said to have been involved. This is Oliver's Ait, which lies between Kew's railway and road bridges. Over recent years it has led a blameless and rather boring life as a useful site for mending boats and storing the Port of London Authority's equipment, but it is said to have had its hour of glory, when—the legends vary—Oliver Cromwell either withdrew there briefly to discuss his military plans or escaped there from the *Bull's Head* on the north bank via an underground passageway. Historians are sceptical, but signs of what might have been steps were found when the pub was recently rebuilt—and why otherwise should the ait have got its name?

Certainly the Commonwealth had some impact on Kew, as, after the execution of Charles I, Parliament sent its Commissioners to survey the Manor of Richmond to check on who owned what. They noted that 'Kewe Greene was about 20 acres', and that the total of copyhold dues (the equivalent of rents) were about half those of Richmond. They then assessed the size of the estates by checking on what were called Quit Rents— money paid by landholders in return for relief from the old feudal requirements of service to the king. The sums were minute even in those days, but they do indicate how the land was divided:

Earl of Ancram	£1-7-0
Richard Bennet	18-3
Samuel Fawtre	7-10
Mr. Smethier	4-10
Walter Hickman	1-6
11 others	less than 1/-

Yet one wonders how up-to-date the Parliamentary records were. Walter Hickman had been granted the lease of the ferry by James I, and was one of the few Kew residents known to have played a role in the Richmond Vestry, but he had died in 1617, and his Kew property had presumably long been in the hands of one of his three sons. Bennett too was no longer in residence, as he had at this time shrewdly let his property to a parliamentary supporter. (Where he went himself we do not know, but he was back in occupation at the Restoration.) As for the Ancrums, there is a plaintive note added by the Parliamentary Commissioner to the record that Ancrum also owned Stony Close with fishing rights ... 'we not knowing where to find the said Earl'. The said Earl had presumably known when it was politic to disappear!

While Kew Green was gradually acquiring the appropriate characteristics of an English village, another house was being built less than a mile away downriver, in the centre of what would become eventually the largest of the three areas that make up modern Kew. The house was called West Hall. It is still there, almost as little altered as the Dutch House, and with a history every bit as impressive. Its history, however, relates to a very different tradition.

As a name, West Hall is at least as old as Kew, and was subject to far fewer variations in its spelling! As with Kew, the earliest surviving record of the name is from the 14th century. In 1386, it is described as an estate of some 160 acres. At that time it was included in Mortlake Manor, which was owned by the Archbishops of Canterbury, most of whom stayed in Mortlake at various times between the 11th and the 16th centuries. At the end of the 15th century, however, a new subsidiary manor was created for the area—the Manor of East Sheen and West Hall, with its manor house in East Sheen.

The house of West Hall itself was built at the end of the 17th century, probably by the Lord of the Manor, Thomas Juxon, at which time the manor covered at least 300 acres. Since then the

19 Oliver's Ait today.

house has been home to many distinguished families, though oddly never to the lords of the manor themselves. Some of them, however, would live in an equally substantial house that was built next door, very likely also by Thomas Juxon. This second house, just to the west of West Hall, was initially called Brick Farm. It was almost as big as West Hall and would for a time become the more important.

Until the middle of the 18th century, however, the lords of the manor continued to live in East Sheen, and both West Hall and Brick Farm were let out. The rents seem to have been put to good use. An earlier Juxon had built the first almshouses in Mortlake 'for four widows'. His grandson now endowed them further with £8 per annum from the rents of Brick Farm. The implication is that this important endowment was from the rent of the house, but it is possible that it could have been from the rent of the land, which generally was not farmed by the lords of the manor but let out for grazing and market gardening.

This was a highly profitable business. Between 1500 and 1700 London's population had grown from 50,000 to 500,000. With no means of fast delivery, nor of preserving food, apart from the use of ice houses, London retailers needed their vegetables and meat delivered fresh; so they had to be grown and grazed as close as possible to the city.

Nowhere was better than upriver on the banks of the Thames. From here the vegetables grown by the market gardeners could be driven in daily in carts by the gardeners' wives and children. Mortlake and Kew were among the first to specialise in the lettuces, peas and fruit the Londoners demanded.

Meat, however, posed a separate challenge. As fresh meat could only be provided if the animals were driven up to town, and as long journeys from the shires inevitably meant that animals were likely to arrive thin and exhausted, the answer was to fatten them up in meadows close to town. Again Kew and Mortlake were well placed to take advantage of this trade, using their water meadows to fatten up the 'Welsh Beasties', as they were generally called.

So long as London grew it seemed that the manor of East Sheen and West Hall would never be short of work for its tenants, nor the almshouses short of endowment.

20   The garden frontage of West Hall. The bow-fronted extension on the right was added in the 18th century to what is essentially still a 17th-century building.

Restoration Kew

The restoration of Charles II to his throne also ensured the restoration of the landed gentlemen to their Kew estates.

The major estates were still of considerable size, according to the Hearth Tax Returns of 1664. The Hearth Tax was essentially the forerunner of domestic rates. It was of course highly unpopular, especially as the collectors had authority to enter any house to check on the owner's ability to count his hearths. The Tax Returns, however, are a boon to historians, as they give a clear picture of the size and social content of the 17th-century villages.

In Kew, 29 houses had hearths. Compared with other villages there was an unusually large number of big houses and an unusually large number of very small cottages, but very few houses of medium size. There were five substantial houses: Kew Farm (Ancrum's) with 35 hearths (more than any house in Richmond): the Dutch House (Fortrey's) with 26, and Kew Park (Bennett's) with 25; there were also Mr. Mounteney's (on the south side of the Green) with 16 and another with nine.

The last of these belonged to Sir Peter Lely— the first of what would become a long line of famous Kew artists. Lely was also one of the famous trimmers of his times, being the favoured portrait painter both of Oliver Cromwell and of Charles II. He was, according to Pepys, 'a mighty proud man, and full of state'—with good reason: he was so wealthy that he lent money to the king.

His Kew house was only one of several that he owned. It was set just to the east of where the Herbarium stands today. He left the house to his only son, but there were complications. Young John Lely was not only a minor at his father's death; he was also illegitimate. His father, however, had chosen his executors wisely. One of them had influence with the current Lord of Richmond Manor—the Duke of York, who was later to be James II. Strings were pulled, and young John Lely was allowed to succeed—to the great advantage of the village, for Lely was to play a major rôle in adding what was still the missing element in Kew— a church of its own.

21   Sir Peter Lely—an engraving of his own self-portrait.

The Capels of Kew

It is arguable that the Royal Botanic Gardens might never have been established at Kew, had it not been for the marriage of Sir Richard Bennett's daughter to Sir Henry Capel.

It was a brilliant marriage. The Capels were a leading family at the Restoration—Henry had been made a Knight of the Garter in 1660 and his elder brother became Earl of Essex—while Dorothy Bennett herself was a considerable heiress. She was also well connected, her cousin, the Earl of Arlington, being one of the Cabal who ruled Britain under Charles II. Dorothy is still rightly remembered in Kew as a great benefactress, yet it is Henry who has ultimately had the greater impact on the village she loved—simply because he and the whole Capel family were famously devoted to gardening.

In the 17th century gardening was a fashionable pursuit for the fashionable, but with the Capel family it was closer to an obsession. The elder brother Arthur was himself a noted gardener, and two of Henry's sisters were also well known for their expertise—one of them being largely responsible for laying out the gardens at Badminton on her marriage to the Duke of Beaufort.

Henry would later be raised to the peerage and make a name for himself as Lord Deputy of Ireland, where he was to die in 1696, but until then most of his energies were directed towards establishing a garden in the estate his wife had inherited in Kew. Though it was not a botanical garden, it was certainly known for the unusual plants Capel collected. We hear of him paying £40—a very large sum at the time—for two mastic trees from France, and in 1724, long after his death, Mackay referred to the excellent gardens at Kew, 'said to have been furnished with the best fruit trees in England by that great statesman and gardener, Lord Capel'.

We get some feeling for the house and how Capel laid out his plants from the diarist, John Evelyn, who was a regular visitor to Kew during Capel's life. In 1678 Evelyn noted: 'Hence I went

22 Sir Henry Capel—a miniature by John Hoskins.

to my worthy friend Sir Henry Capel, brother to the Earle of Essex: it is an old timber house, but his garden certainly has the choicest fruit of any plantation in England, as he is the most industrious and understanding in it.'

Ten years later Evelyn observed that Capel's 'orangerie and myrtetum are most beautiful and perfectly well kept. He was contriving very high palisadoes of reedes to shade his oranges during the summer, and painting those reedes in oil.'

The 'old timber house', which sounds Tudor in design and could have been the one occupied a hundred years earlier by Dr. Awberry, is long gone; so too is Capel's garden. Both are now covered by the large lawn to the south east of the Dutch House. Unlike his wife, Capel has no marble monument in Kew, but as with Wren it is fair to say of Capel: 'Si monumentum requiris, circumspice'.

The Building of St Anne's

In the 17th century Kew was in one vital respect quite unlike other English villages of comparable size. It had no church. Parochially Kew had always been part of the parish of Kingston, within the diocese of Winchester. This may have suited the diocese, but it was extremely inconvenient for the residents. No one wanted to travel the five miles to Kingston church. Even a journey of a mile to Richmond was out of the question for the vast majority.

The reason for this peculiar situation lay in the peculiar way in which Kew had developed in Tudor times: there was no single squire around whom an independent parochial organisation might have grown—just a number of powerful nobles who probably spent only a small proportion of their lives in Kew. (In 1522 a chapel had been licensed at Kew Farm when the Byrkis family lived there, but it seems to have been simply for the family's use, and was anyway discontinued in 1534.)

It was not until 1710 that a group of local worthies decided that the village should have—if not a church—at least a chapel of its own. To show how serious they were, they promised contributions. The first list of subscribers, dated 18 August 1710, constitutes an interesting group, as almost every one was either a major landholder in the village at the time or would be in the future.

Richard Levett	£21.10
Chris Appleby	£10.15
Sir Chas Eyre	£20.00
Thos. Howlett	£10.00
Leigh Blackwell	£10.15
Wm. Cox	£10.00
John Lely	£10.15
Arthur Nixon	£10.00
John Murden	£10.15
John Martin	£ 5.00
Jos Murden	£10.00
Thos. Fuller	£ 2.10

Lady Capel added £50 on 1 December 1714

Sir Richard Levett, a merchant, had moved into the Dutch House in 1697 and became Lord Mayor of London in 1700. One of his daughters married a Blackborne, and the Levett Blackbornes were to be major landowners in Kew throughout the 18th century. Despite his initial contribution to Kew

chapel, the Levett family vault and tomb are not at Kew, but at Richmond parish church.

Sir Charles Eyre, one time Governor of Bengal, and Leigh Blackwell had the leases of the two houses built on the site of the old Kew Farm, which had at last given way to redevelopment.

John Lely, John Murden and Jos Murden all had property on the north side of the Green.

Chris Appleby, a barrister of the Middle Temple, and Arthur Nixon both lived on the south side of the Green, Appleby on the site of today's Cambridge Cottage.

Thomas Howlett, whose family would own property all over Kew, lived then on the east side, as did William Cox. Cox and his heirs ran profitable nursery gardens on the old Ware Ground.

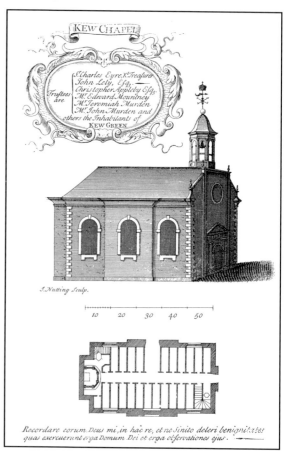

23 Kew Chapel in 1714. Taken from the frontispiece to the charity sermon preached in 1721.

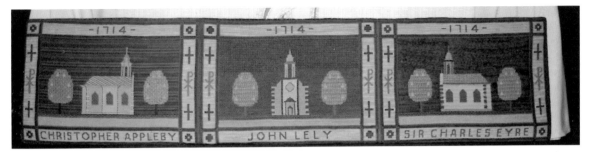

24 The 'founders' of St Anne's, commemorated on one of a set of cushions made by a team of local residents led by George and Kathleen Cassidy, to celebrate its first 250 years.

Thomas Fuller also lived on the east side. He was illiterate—he signed with a mark—but to qualify for a place in this list of local worthies he must have been a man of some substance. In the event, however, both he and John Murden refused to pay their subscriptions for some time. Perhaps there was a disagreement about the building. Whatever the problem, it must have been solved, as John Murden was to be elected Chapelwarden in 1717.

Eyre, Lely and Appleby were clearly the prime movers in the matter. The group petitioned Queen Anne, as Lady of the Manor, for permission, and after due delays she signified her consent, granted a piece of 'the waste' (common) of Kew Green as a site, and offered £100 towards the cost.

Its status was that of a chapel of ease in the parish of Kingston. The building was plain, simple and small. (It did not have to be large. The population was equally small.) The Queen followed the building of the little chapel with personal concern, visiting it on her journeys to and from Windsor.

On 12 May 1714 the little chapel was diplomatically dedicated to St Anne, but it was to have an uneasy first few years. First, the building cost had turned out to be £500 rather than the estimated £250. This was largely solved by the beneficent Lady Capel. She had already given £50. She now gave another £50, and then, when there was still a shortfall in 1719, she headed the list of final subscribers to extinguish the debt.

However, money on its own could not correct another more worrying problem—the behaviour of the chapel's first curate, Mr. Thomas Fogg. In 1717, the Bishop of Winchester received a letter signed by most—but significantly not by all—of Kew's leading citizens listing Fogg's faults: Mr. Fogg did not live in Kew, but only stayed at lodgings there on Saturday nights; Mr. Fogg did not catechise the children; Mr. Fogg kept the collections rather than give them to the poor; Mr. Fogg did not ring the bell 30 minutes, but only some 10 or 15 minutes, before service and 'tho several of the Inhabitants are using their utmost care and Speed to get into the Chappell before the service begins and are in Sight of the same yet such extreme hast is used in reading that the said curate gets into the First Lesson or Psalmes and most commonly beyond the confession and Absolution before 'tis possible for the Inhabitants to get into the Chappell'; worst of all, Mr. Fogg was said to read 'the Divine Service in his Boots and Riding Clothes under the Surplice'.

The Bishop responded with firm orders to Mr. Fogg to mend his ways—which apparently he did as there were no more complaints—but it is noticeable that there was one matter on which his Lordship gave no instructions: he gave no order on the subject of Mr. Fogg's 'Boots and Riding Clothes'.

Sadly Queen Anne herself was never to meet Mr. Fogg, nor to worship at the chapel herself. She died within three months of its dedication—unaware that the Royal Family that succeeded her would themselves in time become parishioners of what she called 'My Little Church'.

Royalty Returns

In Tudor times Kew had touched the hem of history; now with the arrival of the Hanoverian kings it was to find itself almost smothered with it. Once again it was Richmond that initially attracted the royal attention though it was not Richmond Palace, which was now falling into ruin, but a more comfortable, *gemütlich*, setting with which the house of Brunswick fell in love. This was the Ormonde Lodge estate, which stretched from Richmond Deer Park along the river bank to Kew ferry, and so was contiguous with the Capels' estate.

The Lodge itself had once been a hunting lodge, built for James I, and then extended by William III. James Butler, Duke of Ormonde, who had transformed it into a fine ducal home, was in his day second only to the great Duke of Marlborough as a soldier. His day however was very definitely over, as on Anne's death he espoused the Jacobite cause, went into exile, to return only in the abortive rebellion of 1715. His brother, left to find a buyer for the Richmond estate, sold it in 1718 to George, the new Prince of Wales and—more significantly—the new Princess, Caroline. It was renamed Richmond Lodge.

25 Stephen Duck, the 'Thresher Poet'.

26 Richmond Lodge by Jan Griffier. The perspective has been somewhat distorted to include Syon House (where the picture now hangs). The Lodge (as can be seen on page 30) in fact stood well back from the river.

Caroline loved the house and grounds. George irritably indulged her obsession. With more diplomacy—and a considerable amount of public money—Robert Walpole, the Prime Minister, did the same. He recognised how much power Caroline would wield as queen. She engaged Charles Bridgman to landscape the grounds, and William Kent to design elaborate follies such as the Hermitage and Merlin's Cave.

Merlin's Cave was furnished with a library and waxwork figures of legendary characters. Caroline employed as keeper of this bizarre building an equally bizarre librarian—Stephen Duck, a rustic poet from Wiltshire who enjoyed fame at that time as 'the Thresher Poet'. After the Queen's death in 1737 Duck took holy orders and was for some years a popular preacher at Kew. In fact he was so popular that at one time he was seen as a rival to Kew's current curate, the distinguished scholar Thomas Morell. However, Duck was appointed instead as Vicar of Byfleet. He drowned in the Thames in 1756, but his daughters lived on in Kew.

In addition to improving the grounds of the Richmond estate, Caroline added to the Lodge, but even so it could not cope with the demands of their family as well as the staff when George succeeded to the throne. Caroline's solution was to expand the estate by acquiring three of the houses down by the ferry: the Dutch House, and the two recently occupied by Leigh Blackwell and Sir Charles Eyre, the last being known from then on as the Queen's House. The Dutch House became the royal nursery for the next three generations, being used successively by her three daughters, Anne, Amelia, and Caroline, her grandson (the future George III), and then by his children too.

27   Merlin's Cave.

28   Thomas Morell, curate of St Anne's—an engraving by Hogarth. Morell was a distinguished antiquarian and author.

Aberrations at Kew

The final list of subscribers to Kew Chapel, led by 'Lady Capell', was concluded by a less familiar name—that of 'S. Mollyneux'.

Samuel Molyneux, as he is usually known—consistency in the spelling of his name was no better than with that of Lady Capel—was secretary to the new Prince of Wales. With a nice sense of timing he had just married Lady Capel's great-niece Lady Elizabeth Capel. It appears that they were then living with Lady Capel at Kew House, the ideal commuting distance from Richmond Lodge. Even more conveniently for Molyneux, Elizabeth was due to inherit the whole estate on the death of Lady Capel.

Dorothy Capel died in 1721. By 1724 Molyneux had redesigned the house, with space for a telescope in the east wing. (His job might be secretary to the Prince, but his hobby was astronomy.) The telescope was supported by some ironwork, which 'was fixed very strongly to a large stack of brick chimneys which were ... part of the house being some three hundred years old'. We do not know what other alterations Molyneux made, but sufficient for Mackay to describe it in 1724 as Mr. Molyneux' 'fine seat'—clearly an advance on what Evelyn had described as 'the old timber house'.

Molyneux had for some time been working with James Bradley, a distinguished scholar, on his astronomical studies. Now, using the telescope in Kew House, they were to make observations from which Bradley would be able to announce in 1729 a major scientific discovery, that of the Aberration of Light.

29 Lady Capel's memorial. This memorial tablet to Kew's major benefactress is set in St Anne's south aisle in which the school she endowed was once established.

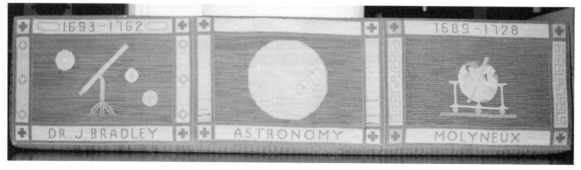

30 The first astronomers of Kew.

A The Dancing Master or Preternatural Anatomist.
B An Occult Philosopher searching into the Depth of things.
C The Sooterkin Doctor Astonish'd.

Cunicularii
or
The Wise men of Godliman in Consultation
They held their Talents most Adroit
For any Mystical Exploit. Hudib.

D The Guilford Rabbet Man Midwife.
E The Rabbet getter.
F The Lady in the straw.
G The Nurse or Rabbet-Dresser.

31 The Cunicularii or Wise Men of Godliman—Hogarth's satirical engraving of St André (third from the right) and his fellow doctors being duped by Mary Tofts.

Sadly, Molyneux himself was not there to enjoy the applause. His luck had come to an abrupt end. In 1728 he fell ill and into the hands of Dr. Nathaniel St André. St André seems to have been primarily a musician and dancing master, but he also practised surgery though without having received any recognised training. George I had appointed him Anatomist to the Royal Family. However, his one claim to lasting fame was that he was persuaded by a certain Mary Tofts, a rabbit keeper of Godalming, that she had given birth to a litter of rabbits. It is uncertain if St André was credulous or corrupt, but amazingly, despite ridicule after Mary Tofts admitted the fraud, he kept his court appointment. However, he seems to have done Molyneux no good, for Molyneux declined and died at a pace matched only by that with which St André subsequently eloped with his widow.

Frederick and Augusta come to Kew

Lady Elizabeth Capel left Kew with Nathaniel St André in 1728. There were no legal proceedings against them, but not surprisingly they did not return. Meanwhile the Capels' garden wilted, waiting for a new owner.

The new owner was a surprise in every way. He was Frederick, Prince of Wales. His father, next door neighbour at the *gemütlich* Richmond Lodge, was now George II. With any other family it might have seemed even more *gemütlich* that his son—until now resident in Hanover—had chosen to live next door. But not with this family. The eldest sons of the House of Hanover were invariably at loggerheads with their fathers. With Frederick, it was even worse. He was not even on speaking terms with his mother. She assumed—perhaps rightly—that he had moved next door simply to annoy her.

Certainly the property was not ideal. John Hampshire, the 'rat physician', caught 500 rats there in a day, and took them to the Prince to show off

his prowess. The building clearly had to be modernised. The Prince decided on the Palladian style—which would result in the house being renamed the White House—and for this he chose his mother's favourite architect, William Kent. His mother, on other matters a not unreasonable woman, decided that this was yet another slight.

Frederick was clearly a difficult son. In Hanover he had liked to roam the streets with his fellow bloods, breaking windows, and playing childish pranks. His choice of mistresses was also tactless, his first being the remarkable Madame d'Elitz. She had already been both his father's and his grandfather's mistress. 'There's nothing new under the sun,' said one courtier. 'Nor under the grandson,' added the wit, George Selwyn. The King felt he was mocked.

Yet on his arrival in England Frederick made a major effort to please the British. He took up racing and cricket. He made good use of

32 *The Royal Coach Crossing the Ferry.* Detail from a painting of Kew ferry by an unknown 18th-century artist.

Molyneux' equipment by studying astronomy. He collected pictures and became a patron of poetry. As a result, he won golden opinions. This however had exactly the wrong effect on his parents, who resented his popularity. Sadly, music, the one taste he shared with his father, was simply the occasion for a further feud: Frederick liked Bononcini, while George liked Handel.

At least they agreed on Frederick's bride. George chose Augusta of Saxe-Gotha, and Frederick enthusiastically backed his judgment— and with good reason. Even the most carping admitted that Augusta had a pleasant expression and engaging manner, though she was, like many girls, somewhat pitted with smallpox. She also had a lot of commonsense, and did her best to calm down the feuds between the two estates.

The young couple spent much of their time in London, but as years went by they gravitated more and more to Kew. Often they would travel up river in the barge specially created for them by William Kent, but clearly they also used their coach, as the ferry receipt book for 1732-7 records the frequent crossing of HRH, as well as the 'Prince's Butcher's Cart'.

33 Prince Frederick's barge. Designed by William Kent in 1732, with carving by James Richards, the barge is now in the National Maritime Museum.

The ferry was clearly very busy in these years. We are told that the Queen's coachman owed 5/, and that the War Office paid 15/- for carrying over and back 41 men and horse. These entries are punctuated by more everyday entries such as '1/- for 2 cowes and 4 horses'. It could be a risky business too: in 1751 a coach and four belonging to a Mr. Latwood was crossing when the horses took fright and leaped into the water with the coach; two horses drowned, but the coachman escaped. At another time the coachman was less lucky. The inquest decided it was his own fault: he was drunk.

Kew in 1734

John Roque, the most fashionable and prolific of the 18th-century cartographers, produced several maps of the Richmond Gardens. As with all his maps, they are rather more decorative and less exact than the Ordnance Survey series that would follow in the 19th century, but his illustrations of the royal houses are invaluable.

Most print makers of the time (see page 37) liked the view from the south of the White House. Roque gives illustrations of both fronts, and indicates that Kent may have made far fewer changes to the north elevation than to the south. He also includes the only picture we have of the Queen's House (previously Sir Charles Eyre's).

In the bottom right-hand corner of the map we can see clearly the relative size and position of the White House and the other royal houses—the Dutch House was only 100 yards from the White House—and how few other houses were built at this end of Kew Green.

The village of West Sheen (on the site of the old Carthusian monastery) lay to the north west of Richmond Lodge; on this map West Sheen is unfortunately obliterated by the right section of the decorative cartouche!

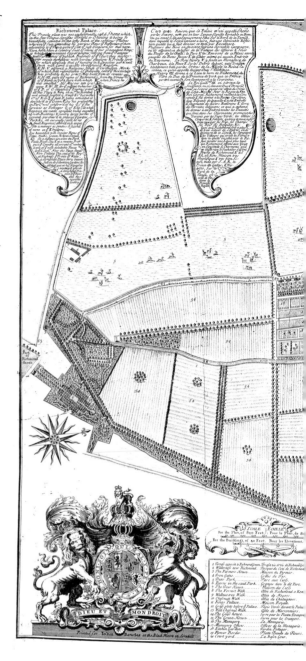

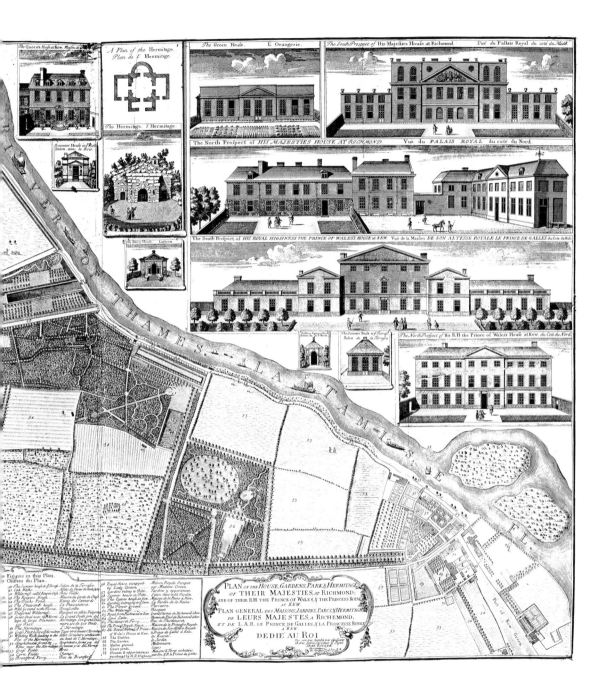

The Quen's House at Kew. Maison de la ...

A Plan of the Hermitage.
Plan de l' Hermitage.

The Hermitage. / Hermitage.

The Green House.   L' Orangerie.   The South Prospect of His Majesties House at Richmond.   Vüe du Pallais Royal du coté du Midi.

Summer House in y Rock
Salon dans le Bois

The Dairy House.   Laiterie.

The North Prospect of HIS MAJESTIES HOUSE AT RICHMOND.   Vüe du PALAIS ROYAL du coté du Nord.

The South Prospect of HIS ROYAL HIGHNESS THE PRINCE OF WALES'S HOUSE at KEW.   Vüe de la Maison DE SON ALTESSE ROYALE LE PRINCE DE GALLES du Coté du Midi.

The Summer House in y Terras.
Salon de y Terrasse.

The North Prospect of His R.H. the Prince of Wales's House at Kew. du Coté du Nord.

PLAN of the HOUSE, GARDENS, PARK & HERMITAGE
of THEIR MAJESTIES, AT RICHMOND;
AND OF THEIR R.H. THE PRINCE OF WALES, & THE PRINCESS ROYAL
AT KEW.
PLAN GENERAL DES MAISONS, JARDINS, PARCS & HERMITAGE
DE LEURS MAJESTES, A RICHMOND;
ET DE L.A.R. LE PRINCE DE GALLES, & LA PRINCESSE ROYALE
A KEW.
DEDIE AU ROI

The First of the Royal Gardeners

Prince Frederick's patronage of the arts was not simply a matter of collecting what he liked: he was a personal friend of poets and painters. James Thomson, a romantic poet renowned for his long poem, 'The Seasons'—then way ahead of its time and now long forgotten—lived nearby, at the Richmond end of the foot road from Kew ferry. Thomson and Frederick used to go for long walks together. Alexander Pope, who lived at Twickenham and was even more renowned, gave the prince a dog to take on these walks. He wrote for its collar what is probably his most quoted couplet:

> I am His Highness' dog at Kew;
> Pray tell me, sir, whose dog are you?

These walks were typical of Frederick's time at Kew. Although he had lived most of his life in Hanover, he rapidly acquired the style of an English country gentleman. He not only followed fashion by gambling large sums on cricket matches; he played in them himself, once captaining a team on Kew Green against another led by the Duke of Marlborough. His passion for games apparently was not restricted to the cricket field and tennis court, as we are told that William Kent's elegant drawing-room furniture suffered from the family games of indoor baseball that the Prince used to organise after dinner.

The greatest of Frederick's enthusiasms however was for gardening—the one taste he shared with his mother, though even on this they could not agree. She was interested primarily on how a garden looked. He was concerned with what it grew: the Kew garden had less room for elaborate schemes of landscaping. He did have an exotic Chinese summerhouse, but he was more interested in exotic plants.

He found two unexpected allies in his hobby, his own young wife, Augusta, and a nobleman he met over a game of cards one rainy afternoon at the races in 1747: John Stuart, Earl of Bute. Between them they had ambitious plans. 'The Prince of Wales is now about preparation for building a stove three hundred feet in length,' wrote a contemporary, 'and my Lord Bute has already settled a correspondence in Asia, Africa, America, Europe, and everywhere he can...'

Frederick was not to see his stove (greenhouse) built. In 1751 he caught cold and died. Two causes

35 *The Music Party* by Philip Mercier, 1733. This picture of Prince Frederick with his sisters Anne, Caroline and Amelia in the garden of his White House poses a puzzle. The sisters, all of whom at various times lived in the Dutch House (seen in background), were said to dislike their brother intensely. Why then did he commission this picture (along with another version which is set inside Hampton Court), and why did he hang a picture of Anne in his dining room (see plate 36 opposite)?

were given, each reflecting a different side of his personality. His doctor ascribed his death to 'contracting cold by standing in the wet to see some trees planted'. Horace Walpole, another near neighbour with his little Gothic Castle at Strawberry Hill, said it proceeded 'from a blow with a tennis ball some years ago'.

Frederick's parents provided a disdainfully inadequate funeral, and Prince Frederick is known now, if at all, for lines written on his death by a Jacobite naturally prejudiced against the Hanoverian succession that had brought an end to Stuart rule.

> Here lies poor Fred,
> Who was alive and is dead:
> Had it been his father,
> I had much rather;
> Had it been his brother,
> Still better than another;
> Had it been his sister,
> No one would have missed her;
> Had it been the whole generation,
> Still better for the nation;
> But since it is poor Fred,
> Who was alive and is dead,
> There's no more to be said.

In fact, there is considerably more to be said. From those who now enjoy the Royal Botanic

36 Frederick, Prince of Wales, with the Knights of the Round Table—painted by C. Philips in 1732. This group painting of the Prince's 'dining club' (in the Queen's Hampton Court Collection, but not on display) is the only authenticated picture of the interior of the White House. In the background is a portrait of the Princess Royal by Mercier.

Gardens he especially deserves the occasional libation in his honour. Like other popular, perhaps populist, Princes of Wales, he might have made a poor constitutional monarch, but without his enthusiasm the garden would never have taken the course it did.

The Vestrymen

With the arrival of Prince Frederick, Kew seems to have taken stock of itself, liked what it saw, and settled for a few modest improvements. Royalty up the road might choose to go Palladian with their White House, but the rest of Kew would be happier with a more domestic style of architecture.

By 1745 there were some eighty houses spread around the Green and up Kew Road. One by one the cottages around the Green had been bought up and replaced by houses of a distinctive Georgian pattern. This though was not unusual. Most villages of the time were assuming a similarly solid, sensible air. They had a lot to be solid and sensible about, as more and more local problems were now left to the local community to solve for themselves. Kew in fact was becoming a typical English village, with a typical divide between the classes. It was unusual only in that it had the Royal Family among its parishioners.

It had a comparatively small working class. They worked in service, or as farmworkers or fishermen, their names known now only if they were the subject of some inquiry, such as an inquest into a drowning from the ferry.

At the other end of the economic scale, there were the ladies and gentlemen with money. Some were famously generous, such as Lady Capel, who died in 1721, and the Countess of Derby, who died in 1717. The Countess left 'the mansion house wherein she dwelt' in Kew in trust for the needy of the parish—a trust that is still active in Kew. (The Derby land was once Suffolk property which the Countess had inherited through marriage.) Others, however, were apparently less bountiful. A 1724 survey of the Winchester diocese, which recorded that Kew had 200 souls, also identified the VIPs: the Rt. Hon. Lord Delaware, the Rt. Hon. Countess of Bouchinbourg, Sir John Hubbard, Sir John Brown (who had bought the Derby property), Lady Conway, George Harrison, the Hon. S. Molyneux, and Sir John Eyre. At a time when communities depended on the generosity of the rich, it is striking that only the

37 *Kew and Strand Green.* This oddly titled print gives a rare if distorted picture of Kew riverside before the building of the first bridge. The castellated building in the background is Syon.

38 *The Augusta* by William Woollett. Given to Prince George on his 17th birthday, this swan boat was built by John Rich of Covent Garden Theatre. Around the lake (now the site of the Palm House) are the Temple of Arethusa (since rebuilt and resited), the White House and the Orangery.

last three are known to have contributed to the coffers and the life of the village.

These three gentlemen worked alongside the third and most important class, the middle class, an interesting mixture of lawyers, publicans, tradesmen and builders, who, along with the local clergyman, would effectively be responsible for the administration of Kew throughout the next two centuries.

Local government in Britain at this time approximated—by chance rather than through the adoption of any political philosophy—to the democracy pioneered by the Greeks over two thousand years before. Each man of property was expected to undertake, without reward, a fair share of parish duties. In Britain, this was organised via the Vestry, which was essentially a parochial church council. Therefore, the needs of the established church were included within the overall needs of the community, an arrangement that would eventually lead to conflict and reform.

Appropriately, one of the first names we encounter in the minutes of Kew Vestry's very incomplete records is a gardener, John Dillman.

Dillman was in charge of Prince Frederick's garden. He and his sister had come, as had Frederick, from Germany, though at a far younger age. Like Frederick too they had settled immediately into the English way of life. Both had married within Kew, John marrying Mary Biggs, and his sister Anne marrying Thomas Dawney, the parish clerk, a man of some importance as he acted as assistant to the curate.

It is difficult to say whether brother or sister in the end had the greater influence on Kew. John became its major landowner, but died childless. Anne played no great part in the village herself, but within four generations her direct descendants included 14 artists, all distinguished in their chosen careers.

In the Vestry minutes of 1741 we find John Dillman asking for relief from his post as Overseer of the Poor. He explained that he had to travel abroad on behalf of his employer—perhaps to collect plants. By this time Dillman would probably have worked his way through the two more junior posts of Headborough, and Constable (both traditionally Manor Court appointments, and then concerned with controlling the behaviour of persons within the parish). As Overseer for the Poor he would have been responsible for collecting the poor rate from householders and distributing it as required. He would then have been next in line for Chapelwarden (chairman of the Vestry).

Although the minutes repeatedly record concern over the lack of men to fill the posts of responsibility, Dillman was allowed his exemption. He did not escape for long, however, as later in the 1740s he was one of those responsible for collecting window tax along with Howlett, a local builder, and West, who owned the inn on Brentford Ait.

Dillman seems to have been a spectacularly successful gardener, his salary going from £50 in 1730 to £700 on his retirement in 1752. By then he had also bought so much land that at one stage he sold fields to his employer—and he was one of only six Kew gentlemen paying tax on their chaises, the 18th-century version of the road tax. When he died childless, he left to his niece, Anne Engleheart, and to her son, what would be one of the major Kew estates.

The Launch of the Botanic Gardens

Lord Bute was known not only for his enthusiasm for gardening, but also for the elegance of his legs. Horace Walpole wrote that when Prince Frederick was alive and wanted to be alone with his latest mistress, he would bid Princess Augusta to walk with Lord Bute, and that when Frederick was dead they walked more and more, in his memory. To be fair—and fairness was hardly one of Walpole's strongest suits—they did something infinitely more substantial: between them, Augusta and Bute carried Frederick's plans for a botanic garden into fruition.

First they engaged William Chambers, partly to act as drawing master to Augusta's eldest son, Prince George, who had moved into the Dutch House, and partly to redesign the White House grounds. These were now effectively divided into three parts by a large lake that covered the ground now occupied by the Palm House itself and included the lake in front of the Palm House. South

39 The Great Stove. Kew Gardens' first great glasshouse was planned by Prince Frederick, and built after his death by William Chambers.

40 The White House (later the first Kew Palace). This print by Joshua Kirby shows the house after it had been rebuilt in Palladian style by Kent.

of the lake were two meadows for sheep, surrounded by ha-has. North of it were the White House and its lawns. To the east of it lay the botanic garden. To add variety to the flat landscape, Chambers created little hillocks, most of them topped by follies built in fashionable classical style.

The botanic garden itself was strictly functional. It was walled, and about nine acres in size. In addition to the exotic plants collected by Bute, it included an arboretum, most of the trees coming from the Duke of Argyll's collection. (Argyll who died in 1761 was related to Bute.) The *Sophora Japonica* (now bent right over), the *Ginkgo biloba* (Maidenhair Tree), and the *Robinia pseudacacia* (False Acacia) may all be originally from Argyll's garden in Whitton.

Although many outsiders feel that Frederick— or even Henry Capel—should be given the credit for creating the botanic gardens, its official foundation date is 1759. It was the date that the young Scots gardener, William Aiton, was persuaded to take charge under the overall direction of Lord Bute. He had been working at the Chelsea Physic Garden. (The Chelsea, Oxford and Edinburgh botanic gardens all pre-date Kew.) By then work had begun on the Great Stove that Prince Frederick had originally planned. Though he was not there himself that year, he had left his mark.

41 Augusta, Princess of Wales, mother of George III— an engraving from the original by Sir William Beechey.

The First Selwyn

While Dillman and his fellow Vestrymen on Kew Green were conscientiously carrying out the duties expected of them, a neighbouring landowner was making his mark on local government in a more radical manner. This was Charles Selwyn.

Selwyn's father had been a career officer in the earliest days of the regular army, and Charles had obtained his commission at the age of three. (His elder brother apparently showed superior promise, being commissioned at four months!) Both brothers fought with distinction under Marlborough, and then resigned in 1715 to work as MPs for the Walpole administration.

Charles Selwyn settled at West Sheen, on the site of the old Carthusian monastery. He had moved to Richmond as, like Molyneux, he held a post at the court of Queen Caroline. He married a local heiress, Mary Houblon, and shrewdly bought most of the land that now lies between the Royal Botanic Gardens and the railway.

For many years he and his brother John worked together in support of a number of philanthropic causes, only to fall out in the end over Walpole's own lack of radical commitment. In frustration, Charles moved to the patriot party favoured by Prince Frederick. Shocked by this disloyalty, his brother insisted that Charles give up the family's 'rotten borough' seat in favour of his own son George, a man known for cynicism rather than philanthropy.

Being forced out of parliament in this way was less of a blow than it might have seemed, as Charles had long ago decided that his energies were wasted in parliament and should instead be devoted to the reform of local government in Richmond.

He had been for many years an unusually conscientious JP in the Surrey Quarter Sessions. JPs were then responsible not only for dispensing justice but also for ensuring, either directly or via

42 The Richardson 1771 map of the Manor of Richmond, showing the development of Kew Gardens and the growth of the Engleheart and Selwyn estates up the Kew Horse Road (Kew Lane).

the Vestries, that roads were repaired, that the Poor Law was administered, and law and order enforced. He was also on the Richmond Select Vestry, which was notoriously ineffectual. The system, he saw, was not working as it should.

It is uncertain how far Selwyn was motivated by a passion for radical reform, and how far by self-interest, but his initiatives certainly led to a radically democratic solution. He revived the powers of the neglected Parish Meeting, which then passed a resolution that 'it had a natural right to look into the accounts and disposal of all such monies as are levied upon them'. This they then did, criticising the JPs (including Selwyn himself!) for failure to buy fire engines. From then on, in Richmond this broad-based public meeting elected officers (Selwyn often being elected Church-warden), who transformed the local administration, employing watchmen (forerunners of the police force), and building a workhouse for the poor. Selwyn died in 1749, before his work was complete, but in time the system of local democracy that he pioneered would be praised by other reformers and copied elsewhere in the country.

Prince George and the Fair Quakeress

On Prince Frederick's death, Lord Bute not only became Augusta's closest friend and confidant. He became a second father to her eldest son, the new Prince of Wales—far closer and more respected than any real father in this royal family. Prince George wrote him long letters in support of Bute's belief that the Prime Minister, William Pitt, was destroying the country in his pursuit of absolute victory in the long war with France. He wrote even longer letters asking for his advice on whom that he should marry, most famously in 1759 on whether he might marry the pretty Lady Sarah Lennox. Bute advised he should marry a German princess, and George declared that he was prepared to lose his love rather than his friend.

In view of this exchange of letters, the extraordinary events that are believed to have happened at St Anne's Chapel in Kew in 1759 appear even more extraordinary. There is evidence that in that year St Anne's could have witnessed the first marriage of the young Prince of Wales who was to rule the country for sixty years as George III—and, if it did, then the implications are clear: the King was a bigamist and was succeeded by those who had no right to the throne.

Not surprisingly the evidence for this 'first marriage' has never been legally accepted, but it was presented in a court of law and it is available for all to see in the Public Record Office. What it indicates is that on 17 April 1759, just a year before he succeeded to the throne, Prince George married Hannah Lightfoot in Kew Chapel in the presence of William Pitt and Anne Taylor. It was a modest setting for so momentous a marriage, but then it was a very modest wedding. Clearly it was intended that the marriage remain secret—not just from the press—but from the Prince's family.

The bride was a young Quakeress, with whom the Prince had fallen in love some years before. Apart from her religion, there was nothing unusual in such a liaison. All young princes had mistresses. What was unusual though was that Hannah insisted that they marry. Even more unusual was the choice of witnesses.

The wedding was not entered in the St Anne's registers, but then it was not conducted by the curate, but by the Reverend Dr. Wilmot. Wilmot was a distinguished scholar, and a friend of Pitt.

43 The certificate of the marriage between Hannah Lightfoot and Prince George at Kew Chapel, as exhibited at the Ryves trial in 1866.

According to the same batch of evidence, Wilmot was already an expert in clandestine royal weddings; he had apparently just married his own daughter to Prince George's brother, the Duke of Cumberland! After the wedding, we are told, Hannah was spirited away to live in seclusion until her death in 1765, having already given birth to three children by Prince George.

The whole story is so bizarre that most 19th-century historians chose to dismiss it, allowing only that Hannah might have been George's mistress. It is easy to see why they were sceptical. To believe the story, one has to believe that Prince George was infinitely more devious than he appeared, and Pitt far less. George used to call Pitt 'the snake in the grass'. Why then should Pitt have involved himself in such a delicate situation?

Yet the documentary evidence is impressive. It emerged long after George's death, in 1844, when his granddaughter was on the throne. How the documents came to light is explained on page 88. At the time they were dismissed by the Lord Chief Justice as forgeries, yet there is circumstantial evidence to suggest that the documents are quite genuine. Certainly it is clear that Queen Charlotte, George's 'second' wife, whom he married with some state two years later, believed the story, as she insisted on an extra private wedding ceremony in 1765—the year of Hannah's death.

None of this would perhaps have mattered very much, were it not for Hannah's three children, all given the surname of Rex. Two of them lived and died in some obscurity, but the eldest, George Rex, lived in Kew as a young man, and was much favoured by the King. Then without explanation he was suddenly sent out to South Africa. Here he established a considerable estate and dynasty of his own, and never returned to England. Although he kept personal mementos given him by George III, and was generally believed in South Africa to be his son, he resolutely refused to talk either about his parentage or why he was so summarily sent abroad. It was—like the marriage in St Anne's—to remain a mystery.

44 John Stuart, 3rd Earl of Bute—an engraving from the painting by Allan Ramsay, commissioned in 1758 by the Prince of Wales.

The First Bridge

Richmond Palace is uniquely famed for being the site of Queen Elizabeth's death, but Richmond and Kew are equally famous for the dramatic receipt by two successive kings of the news of their accession. George II was at Richmond Lodge when Walpole arrived breathless in the middle of the night to tell him of George I's death, only to be greeted with a typically apoplectic, 'Dat is one big lie!' It was not. Then 33 years later George II's death was in turn announced rather more delicately to his grandson in the middle of Kew bridge. On this occasion the new king decided that his horse had diplomatically sprained a fetlock, and quietly returned home to seek advice from Bute.

The bridge was also new. It had been opened the year before, just in time for George to celebrate his 21st birthday by being the first VIP to cross it.

Like most bridges it had not been approved without a battle from other interested parties, but in this case the builder had prepared his ground carefully. He was Robert Tunstall—a Brentford businessman, who wisely had links with influential men in Kew. His brother Thomas had already settled there, and was among the wealthier residents, as in 1757 he was one of only five people assessed for paying duty on his silver plate. Perhaps it was thanks to him that there were no significant objections against the bridge in Kew.

Nor were there any complaints from those who ran alternative services. Tunstall himself owned Kew ferry. In fact, he owned two Kew ferries, though it had taken his family a hundred years to achieve this. The first initiative had been taken by a Parliamentarian Tunstall who had taken over the royal ferry in the days of the Commonwealth, only to lose it at the Restoration. Undeterred, the Tunstalls established a rival ferry based on their limekiln business further downstream. This ferry, called Powel's ferry, also offered attractive terms for pedestrians. Not unnaturally the owner of the royal ferry complained that the Tunstalls were infringing his rights. The Tunstalls responded by buying him out, so gaining a monopoly of the business.

Tunstall's first plan was to build a bridge on the line of the historic royal ferry. Parliament agreed, but was later persuaded by the bargemen that this would restrict river traffic. Right, said Tunstall, I

View *of the* Town *and* Bridge *of* KEW, *in* Surrey.

45 The first Kew Bridge, in the 1760s.

shall put it on the line of my lower ferry. Parliament agreed a second time, and that is where the first bridge, and its successors, were to go.

This first bridge, a wooden structure built by John Barnard, was the only bridge then between Fulham and Kingston, and it was sensationally popular, though none too cheap. The tolls were:

'For every Coach drawn by 6 or more horses, 2/–; for the same drawn by 4 horses, 1/6; for the same drawn by 2 horses, 1/–; for 1 horse, 8d.; for every Baker's Cart drawn by one horse, 6d.; for every led horse, or ass, 2d; and for every foot passenger ½d.' On the first full day of business 3,000 people crossed—not a bad start for Mr. Tunstall.

The Early Artists of Kew

Wherever there are kings or gardens, there will be artists; so it is hardly surprising that Kew has attracted painters from all around the world. What is unusual though is that so many of them were the most distinguished in their chosen fields.

Jeremiah Meyer (1735-1789), miniaturist to Queen Charlotte and George III, is buried in the graveyard of St Anne's. Meyer had a house built almost exactly on the site of the Lelys' house. Though German by birth, like many of the fashionable artists that followed in the train of Britain's Hanoverian dynasty, he was educated in England, and became, along with his Richmond neighbour, Sir Joshua Reynolds, a founding member of the Royal Academy. He was at the centre of an artistic clique who lived in and out of each other's houses around Kew Green, which attracted not only painters, but also the leading musicians of the day. Meyer's house overlooked what we now know as Ferry Lane. At the time it was called, in his honour, Meyer's Lane.

46 Sir William Chambers—a miniature by Jeremiah Meyer, now in the National Portrait Gallery.

47 The Orangery, Chambers' own great artistic achievement.

48 *Perdita*—a painting of Mrs. Robinson by Thomas Gainsborough, commissioned by the Prince of Wales, and now in the Wallace Collection.

49 *The Last Supper* by John Zoffany, now in St Paul's Church, Brentford. Judas Iscariot—the Kew vestryman—is third from the right.

Thomas Gainsborough (1727-88), one of Britain's greatest painters, painted some of his best paintings in the village, and was favoured both by George III and his sons. For many years he stayed intermittently with his friend, Joshua Kirby, who like him had come from East Anglia. Kirby, the less talented, had moved to Kew to become the drawing master to the royal family. Even after Kirby's death Gainsborough continued to visit Kew, staying in a house probably rented by his daughter close to the church.

Although he never owned a house in Kew, Gainsborough chose to be buried there. His modest tomb—now, with its raised stone and railings, somewhat less modest than he intended—can be seen on the south side of St Anne's. Appropriately it is alongside that of his friend, Joshua Kirby.

John Zoffany (1725-1810) is also buried at St Anne's, with which he seems to have enjoyed a somewhat stormy relationship. An immigrant, born Johan Zoffanij, he first made his name as a theatrical painter, much patronised by Garrick; he then made a fortune out of his portraits of the royal family. However, his lifestyle was so extravagant that he had to go off to India to make himself another fortune. One of his more famous pictures there, somewhat surprisingly, was a *Last Supper*, and on his return George III suggested that he paint another one for St Anne's.

This was not to be one of Zoffany's best works, but it is one of his most interesting. His choice of models was characteristically eccentric. Most of the disciples were appropriately local fishermen—all of whom would be known from then on by their apostolic names!—but as St Peter he cast himself, as St John his own young wife, and as Judas a prominent member of St Anne's Vestry—a lawyer with whom he had quarrelled over making his will. (He had played a similar trick in his Indian painting.) When St Anne's refused to pay unless he agreed to repaint the figure, Zoffany gave the painting to St George's, Brentford. It is now in St Paul's, also in Brentford.

Bute and Augusta

George III's decision to turn back to Kew on the news of his accession was typical. George never felt comfortable in London, and for the 60 years of his reign—or at least for those years before he became too deranged to rule—he tried to direct his kingdom so far as possible from either Kew or Windsor. He also tried—but only for the first few years—to direct it by, with, and from the gospel according to Lord Bute.

Sadly for George and the kingdom, Bute was less able a politician than he was a gardener. At the accession, Pitt was Prime Minister, but he very soon resigned in the face of the determination of King and Bute to pursue a peace policy. Bute had to take over himself, though he had few political allies and even fewer political skills. The peace policy was so unpopular that at the next Lord Mayor's Show the cheers for Pitt far exceeded those for George, and were matched in volume only by the boos for Bute.

Bute was now reaping the whirlwind of suspicion that had been blown up long before by those who had criticised the way the King had been educated. Most of the press and politicians were London based. They despised and distrusted the rustic setting and values inculcated in George by Augusta and Bute. The pamphleteers of the time,

far more outspoken than the gutter press of the 20th century, harried them with imputations of adultery.

In 1763, the King reluctantly agreed to release his beloved mentor from the agonies of being Prime Minister. With considerable relief Bute returned to gardening, but the attacks continued until he was forced to leave Kew. Eventually he would die as the result of a fall from a cliff, appropriately in pursuit of a rare plant. By then, however, with the support of Bute and the Princess, Aiton had expanded the botanic garden, and Chambers had completed his landscaping of the Kew estate. In all, Chambers had had a hand in some 23 buildings, of which only six survive today: the temples of Arethusa and Bellona (both since resited), the temple of Aeolus (since rebuilt by Burton), the Orangery, the Ruined Arch and the Pagoda.

The Pagoda is probably the building Chambers would have most wanted to survive, as it reflects his deep interest in Chinese art. Yet sadly even this spectacular folly does not survive exactly as he built it. It was originally decorated with eighty dragons, covered with coloured glass and with bells in their mouths. They have all gone. It is not certain where, or why, they went, but the belief is that they paid off some of George IV's debts.

50 'A view of Lord Bute's erections at Kew'. This engraving, with explanatory notes, was first published in Horne Tooke's satirical *Petition of an Englishman*. It was intended to show how Bute could have visited the White House (A) from his study (I) unobserved from the house (H) 'in which his family lived'. Quite incidentally it gives an excellent picture of the houses on the Green.

51 The Temple of Pan. One of Chambers' finest follies, this was built in 1758.

52 The Alhambra, Pagoda, Mosque—all built by Chambers between 1758 and 1762. The Mosque stood on the hillock now occupied by the Japanese Gateway. This 18th-century print shows the Pagoda's original ornamental dragons.

The Last Days of Richmond Lodge

Before his accession George III had lived at the Dutch House (at that time called the Prince of Wales' House), but as King he initially settled in Richmond Lodge, leaving his mother in charge of the Kew estate. In the first years of his reign he was naturally preoccupied either with matters of state—most of which went awry until he accepted the easy answer of handing back power to Pitt—or with matters domestic, which went far better, as his marriage to Charlotte of Mecklenburg-Strelitz, despite her notoriously unfashionable looks, was productive and apparently happy.

It was not until 1764 that he began to indulge in what would become an almost obsessive preoccupation with reorganising his estate. First, he employed 'Capability' Brown, the most fashionable landscape gardener of the day, to redesign the grounds of Richmond Lodge. Brown began with the pleasure gardens, pulling down Queen Caroline's famous follies, the Hermitage and Merlin's Cave, and creating, with the help of soldiers from the underemployed royal guard, what we now know as the Rhododendron Dell. Elsewhere, as George was particularly interested in farming, Brown made space for cattle and sheep, using the ha-has that first Bridgman and then Chambers had favoured. In pursuit of sufficient grazing, the village of West Sheen was swept away, along with acres of the old pleasure gardens.

At the same time, the King began to take advantage of the change in traffic flow that had followed the building of the bridge. The old ferry was now lightly used, while the Horse Road (Kew Road) was proving inadequate for the vehicles that crowded along it. The King agreed to widen and resurface the Horse Road, in return for closing the other road to Richmond which had run from the ferry along the riverbank and past the gates of Richmond Lodge. At the same time he repaired and renewed the towpath itself.

53 Richmond Lodge by Ricci.

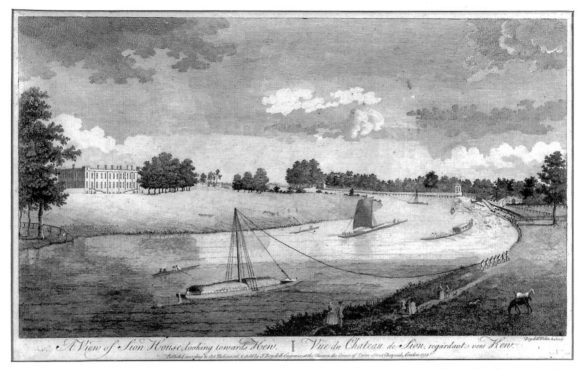

54 Kew's river bank in 1750. This print, with Syon on the left and the terrace of Richmond Lodge on the right, includes a rare scene of halers towing a barge.

55 Kew Observatory, built by Chambers for George III to view the Transit of Venus in 1769.

In those first years of his reign George was less eager than his mother to commission buildings, his first—and ultimately one of his most substantial— being Kew Observatory, which was built on the site of West Sheen. George was fascinated by astronomy and wanted to view the Transit of Venus which was due in 1769. To build the Observatory, he employed his mother's favourite architect, William Chambers. At the same time, as his family was by now rapidly increasing, he asked Chambers to produce designs for a new Richmond Lodge.

Plans were agreed, and foundations for a new palace were dug scarcely sixty yards from the Lodge, but then in 1772 George changed his mind—for two reasons. First there were difficulties over buying a piece of land that was essential for the new palace—Richmond Vestry, though otherwise cooperative, were unwilling to sell. Then his mother fell ill and was clearly dying. A move to the White House at Kew, close as it was to other royal properties such as the Dutch House and the Queen's House, might be a cheaper solution than building a new palace. At her death, Chambers was commissioned to expand the White House, which now became Kew Palace.

As artists still preferred the southern view of the White House, we do not know exactly what changes he made but, as the extension cost over £9,000, they must have been considerable. Meanwhile, the overcrowding was eased by immediately moving the two oldest boys across the way to the Dutch House—the third generation of royal children to use it as a nursery.

George and Charlotte

For George and Charlotte, their first ten years at Kew provided the kind of domestic idyll that they had hoped for, but sadly would be unable to maintain for long. It was, admittedly, a fairly Spartan idyll. Not everyone—and certainly not most of their children—approved of the regime the King and Queen established. The Queen herself, we are told, saw her younger children 'bathed at six every morning, attended the schoolroom of her daughters, was present at their dinner, and directed their attire when not publicly engaged'. The boys were parked either in the Dutch House or in houses round Kew Green with retinues of tutors, governesses, chaplains, and royal physicians, to whom discipline was delegated. Only occasionally did their parents intervene, either to sack employees for mistreating the princes, or, more oddly, to order that one or other of the children needed an extra thrashing—on one occasion 'for asthma'!

The whole operation was a major feat of organisation, as there were eventually 15 royal children. George Selwyn described a procession of coaches 'each stuffed with royal children, like a

56 George III and Queen Charlotte walking in Kew Gardens.

57 The Dutch House—an engraving from the original by Paul Sandby, with the royal children in the foreground, the two eldest of whom were then living in the Dutch House.

cornucopia with fruit and flowers'. These flowers would eventually grow wild, but at that time they presented a charming extra attraction for what was already becoming a fashionable day out from London—a visit to Kew.

The liveliest reports of life in Kew at this time come from the memoirs of Mrs. Papendiek, who was first a playmate of the royal children and then Assistant Keeper of the Wardrobe to the Queen. Allowing for a certain prejudice—the Queen was her godmother—and an even more certain loss of memory—Mrs. Papendiek wrote her memoirs in the 1830s—they give a colourful picture of this rustic royalty.

Kew now became quite gay, the public being admitted to the Richmond Gardens on Sundays, and to Kew Gardens on Thursdays. The Green on those days was covered with carriages, more than £300 being often taken at the bridge on Sundays. Their majesties were to be seen at the windows speaking to their friends, and the royal children amusing themselves in their own gardens. Parties came up by river too, with bands of music, to the ait opposite the Prince of Wales's House. The whole was a scene of enchantment and

delight; Royalty living amongst their subjects to give pleasure and delight.

And on the whole it also gave delight—and profit—to the people of Kew, give or take the first recorded complaint from the locals about the parking—in this case that the coaches were destroying the grass on which their animals tried to feed on weekdays. For those who had different ideals, however, the royal way of life was unspeakably dreary. As Thackeray was to describe it later, 'it was kindly, it was charitable; it was frugal; it was orderly; and it must have been stupid to a degree which I shudder to contemplate'.

Stupid or not, it had a real charm, which can still be recaptured. In 1772 at the end of the Richmond Gardens, close to where the Richmond Lodge once stood, Queen Charlotte built—perhaps to her own design—the Queen's Cottage. It is totally unlike the follies built by Chambers. It has no architectural merit. It is simply romantic—a place designed for family picnics, and decorated by the family's own murals. It is here perhaps rather than in the rather bleak surroundings of the Dutch House that we can recapture something of the cosy royal life of the 1770s. It was not Kew's greatest decade, but possibly for George and Charlotte its happiest.

The Gardens Grow

With the death of Augusta, and Bute's retirement from Kew, there was a danger that the botanic garden they had created might have withered away. Aiton was a fine gardener, but he needed enthusiastic employers and he needed money.

His new employers had something to offer, but not enough. Charlotte loved flowers, and George was fascinated by science, but neither was a botanist. Fortunately, though, they knew—and liked—a man who was. This was Joseph Banks.

Banks was a rich man, so fascinated by botany that at the age of 25 he had persuaded Captain Cook to take himself and five other scientists on Cook's first great voyage of discovery in the *Endeavour*. Banks paid their fares himself.

He returned at just the right time for Kew. The King and Queen were impressed by his enthusiasm, and asked him to undertake a similar role to that held once by Bute. He accepted, and for almost half a century he would be effectively Director of their botanic garden.

As he lived much of his time in his country house at Isleworth, he could watch over the garden's progress. Yet his most valuable service was probably the money he spent personally on sending out young scientists to gather plants from around the world. As a result, during those 50 years nearly seven thousand new exotics were introduced to Britain, among them the hydrangea and tree peony.

Banks' collectors not only benefited Kew; they furthered Britain's imperial interests by taking plants from one country to another. The best known of

58   Sir Joseph Banks.

these projects was the despatch of David Nelson on HMS *Bounty* to collect breadfruit from Tahiti and take it on to the West Indies. That voyage, besides making, and unmaking, the names of Bligh and Fletcher Christian, sadly also proved fatal both for the breadfruit and for Nelson. Undeterred, two more Kew gardeners completed the job just four years later. To their credit, the breadfruit flourished, but to little effect. The West Indians preferred bananas.

59   The Sir Joseph Banks Building—built in the 1980s in honour of the first unoffical director of the Botanic Gardens.

Crime and the Christian Church

With royalty using Kew as its home, at least during summer months, the population inevitably increased as fast as the King's own family. The little chapel, built for a hamlet, was now clearly too small to cope. In 1769, Kew was promoted from a curacy to a parish—though until 1788 its vicar was also responsible for Petersham—and the chapel became a church. This splendid promotion, however, did nothing to solve the lack of space. The new church needed more pews.

The King agreed to pay for the work. He chose as architect Gainsborough's friend, Joshua Kirby, who was then the Royal Clerk of Works, and drawing master to his eldest son. Kirby increased the seating by 140, most of the new pews being accommodated in a north aisle. This was balanced by a two-storey extension on the southern side, which provided space for a vestry, a pew keeper's room, a bone store and a schoolroom.

St Anne's, however, was not simply a religious focus for the growing village; it also provided the essential community facilities common to all such villages at the time. It had—and it still has—a lock-up in the cellar. It also had its own stocks

60 Joshua Kirby—Royal Drawing Master and Clerk of Works.

53

61 St Anne's church, as redesigned by Kirby in 1770.

set up beside the church; for this was the century marked by Horace Walpole's claim that highwaymen had 'cut off all communication between villages. It is as dangerous to go to Petersham as it is to Gibraltar.'

Walpole characteristically exaggerated for effect, but the journey to and from London was certainly hazardous. The Papendieks were once held up in Mortlake—and suspected their coachman of conniving with the highwayman,. In 1776 the Lord Mayor of London's coach was also held to ransom. His Swordbearer was with him, but presumably only in a ceremonial capacity, as the highwayman made off unharmed.

Today this might rate as a major crime wave. Yet, though patronised by royalty, and with soldiers billeted beside the Green (next door to the present Director's House), Kew showed few signs of concern and, as if to demonstrate that the stocks were all for show, Kew's own resident robber used to sit down beside them drinking with his friends. His name was Mr. Frame.

'It was a curious state of things,' wrote Mrs. Papendiek, 'He lived on housebreaking and footpad robberies, but we all spoke with him as a friend.' It was more than curious. It was in fact a very practical form of house insurance. Mr. Frame was blunt about it. 'If I can take my beer on the Green, and sit with my neighbours,' he would say, 'I shall take care that no harm happen here.' And it seemed to work. Mrs. Papendiek makes frequent reference to robberies, but never mentions one in Kew.

The Years of Wine and Music

Kew Green in the 1770s and 1780s was a mecca for musicians. George III loved organ music (though he was somewhat restricted in his tastes by an obsession for Handel), and the rest of the royal family also played instruments. The royal concert master had a distinguished pedigree of his own. He was John Christian Bach, grandson of Johann Sebastian, and with other court musicians would practise in houses around Kew Green, attended adoringly by Mrs. Papendiek and other groupies of the day.

Meanwhile there was a yet more urgent beat, from the aits on the Thames, and it was this that began to attract the attention of the young princes; for as their royal houses around the Green turned one by one from nurseries into 'establishments', so by stages did their parents' rustic idyll fade. Where once the stories were of polite young princes posing beside the little gardens that they tended, now the stories were of their doxies and their debts.

According to Mrs. Papendiek, the equerries to the Prince of Wales had not only overlooked the domestic vices and irregularities of their charge when young, but now 'managed his intrigue with Mrs. Robinson, the renowned 'Perdita', while only a lad, by conducting her to and from the ait at Kew through the garden at the back of the house'. The actress and prince met where Elizabeth and Leicester had met two centuries before, probably beneath the same elm. The affaire went no better than its predecessor, and certainly no longer. As always with the new Prince of Wales, it ended if not in tears then certainly in debt, the King having to redeem at considerable cost promises made by his besotted son.

The ait patronised by Perdita, variously named Brentford or Kew Ait, was famous at the time for the entertainment afforded at its inn, also variously named the *Swan* or the *Three Swans*. William Hickey in his memoirs writes in 1780 of having 'dined

62 Hunter House. The central section of today's Herbarium incorporates the façade of Hunter's Georgian house.

63 Kew Green in 1780. Painted by an unknown artist, this illustrates the Green fenced for livestock, and split by the road that then ran past the palace to the ferry.

upon the island off the town of Brentford, where there is a house famous for dressing pitchcocked eels, and also for stewing the same fish.' The West family who owned it were major figures in Kew. The eels made them good profits. The music and gaiety, however, if no problem to the princes in the Dutch House, eventually became a major source of irritation to those who lived in the big house directly opposite the ait.

This house—the basis of today's Herbarium—had been built in the 1770s by Peter Theobald, a pillar of the community. He was apparently so generous to St Anne's, 'helping the poor and contributing towards pay for the minister', that the Kew Vestry wrote off to the Bishop of Winchester asking for permission 'to give him lifetime use of certain seats for himself and his servants'. It was the equivalent of the freedom of the village. Theobald died in 1778. His unmarried and reportedly equally benevolent daughter, who enjoyed the bizarre privilege—afforded then equally

to heiresses, cooks and the keepers of bordellos—of being addressed as 'Mrs', died in 1796. The house then went to Robert Hunter, a prominent London merchant, and was for some time known as Hunter House.

Robert Hunter did not like the noise from the ait. In a complaint to the City of London, which then controlled this stretch of the river, he described the island as 'a great Nuisance to this parish and Neighbourhood on both sides of the river'. It contained a 'House of Entertainment, which has long been a Harbour for Men and women of the worst description, where riotous and indecent scenes were often exhibited during the Summer months on Sundays'. He asked for permission to fill up thereon 'a pond for catching fish' with earth from his premises on the bank of the river. As an act of Grace he was allowed to do so, which effectively spelt the end of the ait as a place of entertainment for anyone apart from Mr. Hunter himself.

The King's Madness

In 1786 the most literate of all the royal watchers joined the royal staff at Kew. This was Fanny Burney. She owed her position to the respect in which her father was held by the King: Dr. Burney was a distinguished organist. The royal family, being kind enough to overlook her reputation as the author of *Evelina*, therefore unintentionally ensured that they had a brilliant writer working within the court at a time when the court would have liked absolute privacy; for sadly, within months of her appointment, the King went mad.

Fortunately for the royal family, Fanny's memoirs were not serialised week by week in the Sunday press. However, perhaps because they were

64   Fanny Burney.

written at leisure, for those with the leisure to absorb their message, they are all the more informative about life in Kew over those dreadful winter months of 1788/9 when King George was at times unable to tell a tree from an ambassador. What made those months even more distressing was that the doctors had no idea of what was wrong, as the King suffered from porphyria, a disease that had not then been recognised.

In Kew, where he spent most of the nine months of this first attack of the disease, the effect was especially traumatic. The King was known for being a kindly gentleman who would walk out along the towpath, accompanied by just a single equerry, or through the village touching his hat to his subjects, and occasionally subjecting them to embarrassingly detailed enquiries about their circumstances. He was liked—even loved—for his lack of ceremony. Now, however, when he went out for walks he was surrounded by doctors and attendants, and occasionally returned in a straitjacket.

This was all at a time of year when generally the royal family would never have been in Kew. The Kew Palace was far too cold and uncomfortable for winter occupation. Yet the King did recover swiftly, and indeed so completely as to mock the very doctors who had held him in straitjackets.

'Why,' he asked the Rev. Dr. Willis, 'did you abandon religion to practise medicine?'

'Our Saviour himself,' said Willis, 'went about healing the sick.'

'Huh!' replied the King, 'but He had not £700 for it.'

George was probably right to be sceptical. The doctors did their best, but they did not cure him— and never could.

Farmer George

George III was an exceptionally unlucky man. Of all Britain's Hanoverian kings, he was by far the most kindly and well meaning—admittedly the competition was not so strong!—yet he was doomed to have the most unhappy life. Almost everything went wrong for him.

Politically, he was inept. As a father, he was fond but foolish. By tragic chance he was prey to an illness so rare that his doctors not only did not know how to treat him, but could not even explain what was wrong. As a result, he was doomed to spend the last years of his life isolated both from a wife he had devotedly loved, and from farming, the one pursuit at which he showed real ability.

George was not only a good farmer. He was also fascinated by science. He wanted to have the best wool-bearing sheep in the land, and was prepared to experiment to achieve his object. In pursuit of this, he imported Merino sheep from Spain in 1788. They were brought to Kew and grazed on the fields created by Capability Brown. Here, on the whole, they thrived.

Fortunately, Sir Joseph Banks, whom George had asked to care for the botanic gardens, was as interested as his sovereign in the breeding of sheep. So when George was less often in Kew—through illness and a growing aversion to a place he associated with his humiliating experiences at the hands of his doctors—Banks kept an eye on the health and sales of the sheep.

It was therefore Banks who authorised the most significant of all the sales of royal sheep. This was in 1804. It was held in a field just beyond the Pagoda, where now there are tennis courts beside the Kew Road. Then, as now, it was divided from the Kew Road by the ha-ha.

The start seemed unpromising. According to the *Agricultural Magazine* for August 1804, 'Lot 1 (a single shearing ram) ....labouring under a temporary privation of sight, which Sir Joseph Banks and Richard Stafford, the King's shepherd, stated not to be uncommon with these sheep at this season ... was knocked down to Capt MacArthur at £6-15.'

It was not a large bid, but it was significant. Captain MacArthur was known to be trying to build up sheep farming in Australia. There was obviously some tension, however, as at this point Sir Joseph publicly 'apprised him that an old act of Parliament stood in the way of exporting sheep from this country'. This was perhaps a little disingenuous on the part of Sir Joseph, as King George's own sheep had originally been smuggled out of Spain, but Banks may have had genuine doubts about the breed's ability to survive in Australia. If so, he was to be proved wrong. The gallant captain, paying attention neither to acts of Parliament nor to the doubtful quality of the flock, continued to buy, managed to export all that he bought, and bred from this Kew stock the sheep that would eventually make Australia's fortune.

'Farmer George' deserves some of the credit. His nickname was coined in mockery by those who resented his dislike of London, but now it is used by some—especially the Australians—as a compliment. He has won recognition at last.

65 *(below)* The King's sheep in Kew Gardens—a drawing by William Woollett. In the background are the temples of Bellona and Aeolus, and the House of Confucius.

The Closure of Love Lane

Some time before his first fearsome attack of insanity, George had initiated further plans to improve his estates. No longer having any need for Richmond Lodge, he pulled it down and decided to merge its garden with that of Kew

66 *(above)* Love Lane today. The Holly Walk in Kew Gardens follows the line of Love Lane, the far end of which in Richmond is still called Kew Foot Road. As the direct route from Kew ferry to Richmond, it is probably the oldest path in Kew.

Palace. To do this he had to persuade both Richmond and Kew Vestries to agree to the closure of the lane that divided the properties. This was the foot road from the ferry to Richmond, commonly called Love Lane.

Although it would take some years before the requisite legislation was brought before Parliament, the two Vestries gave his plan their full support, partly no doubt because he agreed at the same time to hand over Pesthouse Common on Richmond Hill and build there at his own expense a workhouse for the poor of Richmond and Kew. At the same time the Richmond end of Love Lane—still known today by its old name of the Kew Foot Road—was to be improved by the King, and linked to the Horse Road.

For both Vestries, it was an excellent bargain. For over a century parishes had been trying to cope with poverty by a system of Care in the Community that was hardly more successful then than it has been today. It involved the constables doing their best to drive vagrants out of the parish, on the principle that they should go back to whence they came, while the Overseers of the Poor used the poor rate to aid those of their fellow parishioners who were unemployed or unemployable. As most parishes could offer only limited opportunities for work, most of the recipients were chronically unemployed.

In the 18th century more Vestries began to turn to the harsher but more cost-effective solution of establishing workhouses. Richmond had a workhouse in Petersham Road, but it was inadequate, while Kew had a very limited right to send needy cases to Barnes workhouse. A new workhouse on Pesthouse Common would be far more efficient, and better equipped. Also money to defray the cost could be raised by developing the land around it— just as it still is today by the present trustees of the site, the Richmond Parish Lands Charity.

The workhouse was built swiftly and was honoured by a royal visit: convalescing from his first major bout of porphyria, the King decided to make the journey on foot. He was rewarded with a slice of the workhouse's own homemade bread, and was conducted on a tour of the buildings by the proud Master of the Workhouse. Somewhat tactlessly the Master included a visit to the madhouse, where he discoursed at length on the efficacy of straitjackets. We are told that 'His Majesty heard this ill-timed conversation without the least agitation'.

The Second Bridge

There is no evidence of any outcry in Kew over the closure of Love Lane. The influential citizens now used the bridge rather than the old ferry, and the foot road was—like many such lanes—more popular with lovers and malefactors than with those past whose property it ran. Mankind may love a lover, but not on a footpath behind his house. He loves burglars even less—and the ferry and foot road had been notoriously used by robbers from the north bank of the Thames as a convenient route to escape the attentions of the Brentford constables.

Nevertheless the bridge had its problems. It had been closed for two years in 1774 because a boat had damaged one of the uprights, and it was clear that its wooden structure suffered from chronic problems. A new bridge was needed. Luckily there was a new generation happy to take on the challenge of building it. Robert Tunstall, son of the original builder, along with his brother-in-law, John Haverfield, and a carpenter, called John Brown, applied for a licence to rebuild the bridge in stone.

The Tunstalls had made their money from running a limekiln on the Middlesex bank, but by now most of them lived on the Surrey bank, and Robert's marriage into the Haverfield family ensured that Kew would back the venture.

The Haverfields were very influential in Kew Vestry. The first John Haverfield had come to Kew in 1759. A west countryman, and a master gardener, he had been recommended to Princess Augusta by Lord Bute. While Aiton, who was initially his deputy, looked after the botanic garden, Haverfield ran the Richmond Pleasure garden—or what was left of it after Capability Brown had finished his reconstruction. As he did not qualify for a pension, the King had agreed to a lifetime appointment. It was a long one. Haverfield died in office, at the age of ninety.

Two of Haverfield's sons had worked with him, Thomas leaving to succeed Brown at Hampton Court, and John staying to take over from his father until 1795, when Aiton assumed responsibility for what were now twin gardens. (The use of 'Richmond' to describe the pleasure garden, and 'Kew' to describe the botanic garden, eventually fell into disuse, and they were jointly described as Kew Gardens.)

67   The second Kew Bridge, as seen from the ferry in 1791.

68 William Aiton—a miniature by George Engleheart.

69 *Miss Haverfield*—the painting by Thomas Gainsborough, now in the Wallace Collection, of the daughter of John Haverfield II.

John Haverfield II then seems to have joined his brother-in-law in business, while assuming a role akin to lay preacher at St Anne's. (He was described as a 'clerk' in a will of 1814.) This was a time when the freemason movement was first beginning to make its impact on Britain, and it is interesting that among the members of a new lodge launched at Hampton Court in 1785 there were a handful of Richmond notables, no doubt attracted by Thomas Haverfield. They were led by James Sayer Esq, the King's Deputy Steward of the Manor (and effectively agent for all the royal property). Three of the others described themselves as 'architects', two of whom were Tunstall and Haverfield. They were stretching a point. If they were architects, it would not be of the bridge, but of the very successful business that ensued.

The bridge itself was designed by James Paine, who had just completed Richmond Bridge. It was much admired for its elegance, though it would later be criticised for the steepness of its approaches. Like its predecessor, it was a toll bridge, built on the assumption that the entrepreneurs would recoup their investment over the years. In the event they did so handsomely, selling the rights in 1819 just before the Hammersmith Bridge opened.

The account book for the last year of Tunstall's ownership makes interesting reading, as it not only shows how busy the bridge was at the time, but also records the outstanding debts. 'The Queen ... £11-19-8, The Prince Regent ... £19-19-8, and The Duke of Cumberland ... £9-2-6.' Royalty were notoriously bad payers. Those debts might have been one reason why Tunstall sold out!

Sir Richard Phillips' Walk

In 1813 we have a fascinating, detached, view of Kew. This comes from the account written by Sir Richard Phillips of a walk he took from London to Kew. Most of his book is taken up with philosophising over the state of the world, but he also gives vivid pictures of the places through which he walked.

The last stretch of his walk took him from Mortlake, along a footpath through the river meadows. 'As I approached a sequestered mansion and some other buildings which together bear the name of Brick Stables, I crossed a corner of the meadow towards an angle formed by a rude inlet of the Thames.'

Phillips had been walking along the ancient route of the Kew Meadows Path, described back in 1617 as 'the way leading from Mortelake to Kewe ferry'. The mansion he saw was West Hall with various brick buildings behind them. Had he looked more closely he would have also seen—as

we can see in William Harriott's charming painting of 1819—that behind West Hall, and largely hidden from the pedestrian by the high wall, lay the bigger, and even more sequestered, mansion of Brick Farm.

At this time West Hall was let out to a Lt. Harriott, whose wife is better known as the miniaturist, Diana Hill. Brick Farm itself was occupied by the owners of the estate, Mrs. Elizabeth Taylor, and her three daughters. The estate had come to them from Mrs. Taylor's husband, who had inherited it from the Juxons by a circuitous route, due to the failure of previous owners to produce heirs—a chronic problem that would persist with this estate right through into the 20th century. Between them Mrs. Taylor and her daughters shared the Lordship of the Manor and indeed held manor courts as late as 1808.

As he moved on towards Kew Green, Phillips spotted the only other substantial building between Mortlake and Kew Green: 'My attention was

70 West Hall—by William Harriott. This picture, painted in 1819 by the son of miniaturist Diana Hill, illustrates West Hall from Kew Meadows Path, a few years after Sir Richard Phillips' walk. West Hall has hardly changed since then. Behind can be seen the other big house, Brick Farm.

71 The Castellated Palace. In this print of the second—never occupied—Kew Palace, the world of Kew's rushgatherers appears spectacularly untouched by Kew's 'Bastille'.

attracted by the battlements of a new Gothic building, which I learnt, from the keeper of an adjoining turnpike, was called Kew Priory.' He was also told that he could not go in. The only man permitted to visit was the local Roman Catholic priest.

At the time the 'Priory' consisted merely of a chapel, beautifully situated on a lawn, with a room for refreshments, and a library. It had been built for the wealthy Miss Doughty of Richmond Hill, 'for a change of scene in the long afternoons of the summer season. The enclosed space contained about twenty four acres, on the banks of the Thames ... Nothing could be so tasteful as a place of indulgence for the luxury of wealth; but it is exposed to the inconvenience of floods from the river, which sometimes cover the entire site to a considerable depth.'

In view of its use merely as a summerhouse, it is strange to hear that it also had a capacious pheasantry, an aviary and extensive stables. However, it certainly had space for them. This was the old Ware land of Kew, owned in medieval days by the Priory of Merton. Its monks no doubt looked

down kindly on its unexpected occupation by a Catholic chapel.

Sir Richard now came further down the Mortlake Road, then generally called Sand Lane, to be struck by the sight of what most considered King George's craziest scheme—the second palace of Kew. This was in fact dreamt up in 1800, at a time when the King was apparently in remission from his disease. He had decided that he needed a new palace in Kew—not an unreasonable decision in itself, as the current palace was by then beginning to look distinctly dilapidated—but it was the style of palace he chose that was so bizarre. He commissioned James Wyatt to build him a castle.

It was a romantic concept, but totally impractical. It was erected on the riverside, beside the old ferry. A great battlemented gateway faced the river. This opened into a vast forecourt, surrounded by offices, beyond which rose a massive keep containing the main rooms of the palace. Not unfairly it was nicknamed the 'Bastille'. It looked ludicrous, and it would have been quite impossible to live in. Fortunately, no one ever had to, as it took so long to build that the King entered the

72 The Mortlake Road/Leyborne Park crossroads. Painted by a member of the Atwood family of Leyborne Lodge in about 1830, this shows the turnpike house mentioned by Sir Richard Phillips and—even then—that familiar bend in Forest Road.

final long stage of his illness long before it was ready. At that point—in 1811—work was halted. It had already cost half a million pounds.

Architecturally this second Kew Palace was of some interest as it was one of the first buildings to be supported on cast iron columns, but even this proved a disadvantage in the end. When in 1827 George IV decided to get rid of what had become an embarrassing eyesore, he found it could not be pulled down. It had to be blown up.

Meanwhile—perhaps prematurely—George had ordered the removal of the first Kew Palace. As a result, from then on royalty when visiting Kew were reduced to crowding into the little Dutch House. It must have been very uncomfortable. The sons now had their own establishments—most of them well away from Kew—but the daughters still had to be accommodated. In the circumstances, it was fortunate that the Palace kitchen and stable blocks had been kept.

There was, however, in the whole misbegotten redevelopment one redemptive touch—a rare case of royal family sentiment. Prince Frederick was not forgotten. The Palace door panels, marked with his initials, were salvaged from the first Palace and fitted to the Dutch House doors, where they can still be seen.

Kew at War

As Phillips concluded his visit to Kew, he paused to admire an unusual work of art. All along the wall of Kew Gardens, fronting the Kew Road, were painted 800 ships, each of them five or six feet long. They represented the entire might of the British Navy.

Phillips was writing in 1813. This may explain why the gentleman who had painted the ships was waiting confidently beside his work to be rewarded, rather than be clapped into the lock-up for his graffiti. Britain was at war, and for the last decade Kew, like every other community, had been continuously conscious that the country was under threat from Napoleon.

At such times communities were expected to supply a certain number of recruits for the armed services. As in earlier centuries, though, you could buy your way out of your responsibilities. Where once there were 'quit rents', now there were fines. In March 1805 Surrey was short on its contribution of men to the permanent additional force by 1,010 men, and the fine of £20,200 was divided amongst its parishes pro rata. Kew had to pay £22-18-4.

At the same time each parish had its militia, volunteers similar to the 20th-century Home Guard. In 1803 Kew had its own company with the chief gardener as Lieutenant, and John Haverfield as Chairman of the Committee. There were 60 men, with two drummers, two fifers, a fugleman and an armourer.

Meanwhile, there were, of course, regular soldiers stationed in Kew, as there had been for the last fifty years, to defend the King and his family. Their barracks lay next to what is now the Director's House—just beyond Cambridge Cottage. It must have been an idle, tedious posting, as, on the rare occasions that the royal family were attacked, the attacks took place well away from Kew. In the circumstances the soldiers seem to have caused less disruption than they might have done—generally in the inns.

Kew was affected by the war in one further way, unique to Kew. It became a place of refreshment and recreation for emigrés. A large number of the French nobility, who had fled their country in the 1790s, had settled along the Thames. The houses they rented mostly had fine gardens, but apparently Kew had for them a peculiar fascination. Louis XVIII, the king in waiting, used to visit Kew at least once a week. Perhaps, though King George and the rest of the British royal family now visited it only sporadically, Kew retained for him and his relations something they could recognise: the spirit of royalty past.

73 *Military Manoeuvres on Kew Green*, from the watercolour by Thomas Rowlandson.

The Tyrrells

After 1800, the royal watchers of the day have less to say about Kew. Fanny Burney's account ends in 1792 when she resigned as Assistant Keeper to the Wardrobe, and Mrs. Papendiek's memoirs stop in the same year, just before she accepted the same post.

Unexpectedly, however, another diary has survived, though as yet unpublished, giving a vivid picture of life in the village between 1808 and 1810. This was kept by Mrs. Tyrrell, whose husband Timothy was City Remembrancer (lawyer to the City of London). The Tyrrells had two houses. One was in London and the other at no 59/61 Kew Green. She and the children lived mostly in Kew, as it was considered more healthy. Generally this proved true, though one of the children died during these two years, and the rest had to survive the leeches that the Kew doctors prescribed for almost every malady.

On the whole, the Tyrrells had a very jolly time. There were great expeditions by boat upriver to Teddington lock to meet their father aboard the City of London barge, or to Hampton Court to play in the maze. They had two boats of their own. On one of their picnic parties the boys took one and Mrs. Tyrrell followed with the rest of the family in the other. Soon Mrs. Tyrrell spotted the youngest walking disconsolately along the towpath: he had cheeked his elders. He was hidden in the second boat. When they reached the picnic spot, the older boys were ordered to row back and find their brother. Then when they were almost out of sight, he leapt from his hiding place to wave at them in mockery.

Mrs. Tyrrell was a close friend of the Haverfields and a prime mover in organising village parties. On the King's Jubilee, everyone showed their loyalty by hanging out flags. (Mrs. Tyrrell noted meticulously how each house was decorated.) The richer folk planned a big party at the *Rose and Crown*. It was a great success, though the innkeeper got few marks for the standard of the decorations—the ladies had to sort them out themselves—and even fewer for overcharging the company.

As was often the case, Mr. Tyrrell missed this party. He was kept at the office, concerned that there might be a riot. On a previous celebration a Quaker family had been attacked for failing to display adequate flags, but this time nothing untoward occurred. Perhaps in the City, if not in loyal Kew, there was less concern this time over such peccadillos. After all, the poor King himself was not exactly in a party mood.

74 *(right)* The *Maria Wood*—the City of London barge, which for many years was docked at Kew.

75 *(below)* Leigh's 'Panorama of the Thames'. The Kew section of this invaluable topographical work shows the riverbank in about 1830, with the entrance to the dock and the boathouse for the City's barge. The boathouse was dismantled in the early 1900s.

Kew

Kew Church

Kew Bridge

Sardini on the Green

The Indian Queen

The Star

Malt House

Malt House

George IV truncates Kew Green

King George paid his last visit to Kew in 1806, and for the next 12 years all the royal houses around the Green were either let or kept on a care and maintenance basis—with one exception. The Duke of Cumberland, famous for being the most unpopular of all the unpopular royal dukes, retained his establishment at no. 33.

Then in 1818, by bizarre chance Kew found itself at the centre of a crisis over the royal succession. For years the King's sons had been famous for the number of their children, but nearly every one of the children was illegitimate. This of course had no constitutional importance so long as the Prince of Wales' one legitimate daughter, Charlotte, was alive. Her death in 1817 was therefore a disaster. Of the five eldest princes only the hated Cumberland was now likely to produce a legitimate heir.

No one was more horrified than Queen Charlotte. She was a great hater in a family that knew how to hate, and her pet aversion was the Duchess of Cumberland. The errant Dukes of Clarence and Kent were urged to marry German princesses immediately. That summer the Queen was taken ill on her journey to Windsor, and was advised to stay in Kew. So it was there rather than at Windsor or London that Clarence and Kent were married, the ceremony taking place in the little drawing room of the Dutch House, in the presence of their mother. The 'wedding reception' added an equally bizarre, though unexpectedly sentimental, touch. The princesses organised a picnic tea for the family at the Queen's Cottage.

The Queen herself was too ill to attend that last family picnic, and died a few weeks later at Kew. The King, so disturbed by now that he could not even understand that she had gone, died in 1820.

The new King, George IV, had never shown much affection for Kew, and the changes he made there were hardly popular. In 1824 he closed the road that had run for years across the Green and down to the old ferry. With this closure in mind, he had already bought Hunter House, and all the property that lay between it and the Dutch House. Now he enclosed his estate with a fence, which ran across the Green on the line of Ferry Lane. In the middle he built a gate, surmounted with a Lion and a Unicorn, and made a new entrance to the botanic garden by the barracks.

It must have been a period of major disruption for Kew, as the same Act of Parliament that enclosed the Gardens also enclosed most of the riverside land, splitting it up among those who already had

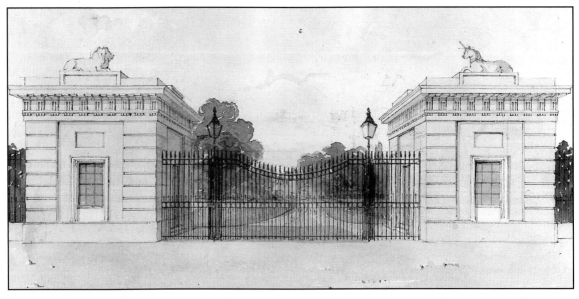

76 George IV's 1825 gate into Kew Gardens, on the line of what was then called Birdcage Walk.

The Family Tree of George III

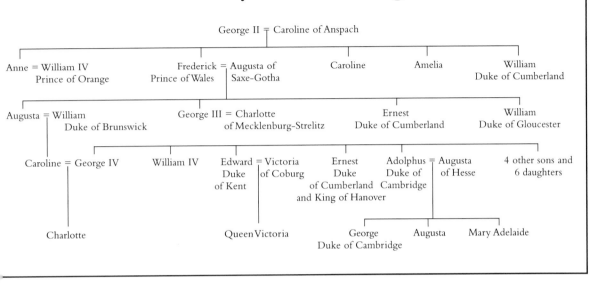

George II = Caroline of Anspach

Anne = William IV
Prince of Orange

Frederick = Augusta of
Prince of Wales | Saxe-Gotha

Caroline

Amelia

William
Duke of Cumberland

Augusta = William
Duke of Brunswick

George III = Charlotte
of Mecklenburg-Strelitz

Ernest
Duke of Cumberland

William
Duke of Gloucester

Caroline = George IV

William IV

Edward = Victoria
Duke | of Coburg
of Kent

Ernest
Duke
of Cumberland
and King of Hanover

Adolphus = Augusta
Duke of | of Hesse
Cambridge

4 other sons and
6 daughters

Charlotte

Queen Victoria

George
Duke of Cambridge

Augusta

Mary Adelaide

77 The Queen's Cottage.

property in Kew and therefore had rights to the meadows. In this it was typical of the 19th-century enclosures. The beneficiaries' names are familiar: Tunstall, Tyrrell, Meyer, Aiton, Selwyn, Engleheart, Doughty, His Majesty. It must have been fine for the great and good, but it is hardly surprising that the new century would be bedevilled with the problems of the poor.

The King's School

The story of Kew's first school begins in the 18th century, but its origins are still shrouded in mystery—possibly because there was very little for those responsible to boast about.

In 1721 Lady Capel left money to endow 12 charity schools, one of which was to be in Kew. Her will stipulated that until its own school was established any of the 12 hamlets could spend the endowment on apprenticing the children of the hamlet, but only so long as they had been educated in one or other of her schools. At first, Kew seems to have sent its poor children to the Capel school at Brentford Butts, and spent the Kew endowment on apprenticeships. Then, in 1742, there was a crisis. For some reason the children could no longer go to the Butts.

The admirable Appleby, who as a leading figure in building St Anne's had been chosen as a trustee of the Capel endowment, pointed out to the Vestry that, as no Kew child was now attending a Capel school, they could no longer use the Capel money on apprenticeships. They must open their own schools for boys and for girls. He announced subscriptions from Prince Frederick and the Princesses, and something from himself.

Appleby acted fast. Two schools were opened in 1742, one for 10 boys, the other for 10 girls. At the same time Appleby succeeded, getting a further endowment of £75 from the trustees of money left by another generous lady, Dame Elizabeth Holford. She had originally left £200 in 1717 for religious education in Kew—it seems to have lost value through lack of use. It is not known where this first charity school was based, but it seems to have closed after three years.

The next effort to provide education was in 1767, when the Vestry decided that the charity boys should be 'educated on Kew Green'. (Apparently they had recently been going again to Brentford.) Once more it is not clear where this teaching took place, but in 1778 the school was moved into the room provided inside the church. This apparently was unsatisfactory as other plans were discussed for moving the school to the parish poorhouse, a church property three hundred yards along the Kew Road which accommodated some of the poor in the 1780s. This plan, though promoted by John Haverfield, as Churchwarden, failed through lack of contributions and, when the Richmond workhouse opened, the parish seems temporarily to have washed its hands of the problem.

The failure to raise sufficient funds must have been an embarrassment to the Vestry, especially as King George III had, like his parents, been contributing an annual sum of at least £21 to the poor of Kew. Also, there was certainly other education available in Kew, though presumably only for those who could pay.

The oddly named Hell House, next to Bute's house on Kew Green, had had a school in 1731, run by a James Smith, and it was again described as a schoolhouse in 1759, 'late in occupation of William Rose, schoolmaster'. Rose was a man of literary tastes, and a friend of Samuel Johnson, who often visited him at Kew. Sadly the great man was unable to enjoy its most attractive feature, for when invited to take a stroll in Kew Gardens he staunchly replied, 'No, sir, I will never walk in the gardens of an usurper'.

In 1777 another small private school was set up in no. 77 Kew Green, with boys being taught in one room and the girls in another. Still later, in 1780, there was yet another private school, run by Dr. Majendie in the Kew Road. None of these, however, catered for the working class, and at the turn of the century, while the destitute were incarcerated at the workhouse, the ordinary poor still went across the river to Brentford.

Some of these children may well have been educated there by the famous Mrs. Trimmer. If so, that was appropriate; for Sarah Trimmer had herself been brought up in Kew. She was the daughter of Joshua Kirby, the friend of Gainsborough, who had memorably allowed space for a schoolroom in his 1770 extension of St Anne's. Sarah became a pioneer of universal education. An admirer of Raikes' Sunday School Movement, she first opened a Sunday School in St George's church (which had been designed by her father). She then moved on to create her 'School of Industry', which trained girls in domestic work. Effectively it was Britain's first attempt at technical education.

Perhaps inspired, or even shamed, by her example, Kew at last got down to providing a Free (Church of England) school of its own. John Haverfield, though no longer Churchwarden,

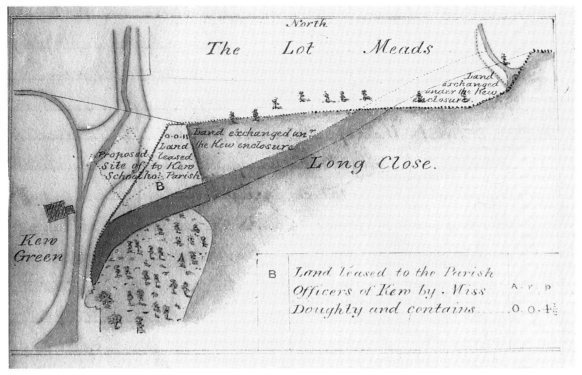

78 The site of the first King's School.

79 The first King's School in 1824.

roused the Vestry to action. In 1810 the school was opened in private premises in Kew Road. (In November the benevolent Mrs. Tyrrell records going 'up Kew Lane to the Children's School and I paid to Xmas for the poor orphans'—which suggests that at that time it catered chiefly for the destitute.) Plans for a permanent site were also drawn up. With an admirable lack of sectarian prejudice, the Catholic Miss Doughty gave some land. The site was between the pond and the river, the design almost as gothic as her own Priory. Boys and girls were to be educated each in their own part of the little building.

Money was solicited widely, and the response was generous, if less than overwhelming. King George IV, feeling perhaps that he owed Kew something in return for what he had so highhandedly appropriated, gave £300, and in 1824 he sent his brother Prince William to open the school. He also commanded that it be called 'The King's Free School'—and since then, with royal permission, the name has changed according to the sex of the monarch to and fro between 'The King's' and 'The Queen's'.

'What the King did pleased all the People'

William IV is generally remembered, if at all, as a bluff, rather eccentric, naval gentleman who reigned for a very short time. In Kew, however, he is remembered also for his affectionate generosity to the village in which he was raised.

As children he and Prince Edward were parked, along with their attendants, in no. 37 Kew Green, then known as 'the house lately occupied by Lord Bute'. Presumably William remembered his childhood there with some nostalgia, as on his succession he immediately gave back to Kew some hundred yards of the Green enclosed by his brother. The elegant main gates designed by Decimus Burton were not erected until 1846, but their positioning had been decided long before by William IV.

Within the gardens, he approved the addition of windows at both ends of the Orangery, which now are marked by his wife's initials. He also commissioned Sir Jeffrey Wyatville to design a temple, now known as King William's Temple, dedicated to the country's achievements in war.

At the same time he robbed two other royal estates to give to Kew. A building Nash had created for Buckingham Palace was set to the right of the path from the Main Gates. It is now known as the Aroid House. He also took a rare sundial from Kensington Palace, marked confusingly not with his own, but with William III's initials, and placed it on the site of the old Kew Palace. The sundial was created by Tompion, the greatest clockmaker of his day. The inscription is unexpected. It commemorates, not Kew Palace and Kew's centuries of royal connections, but the discovery at Kew of the Aberration of Light. William's father and grandfather would have approved of his scientific sense of priorities.

He also extended the church, which had once again been outgrown by its congregation. After Kirby's first substantial extension in 1770, there had

80 The Aroid House today.

81 King William's Temple today.

82 The Tompion Sundial, which marks the site of the first Kew Palace, and commemorates Bradley's discovery of the Aberration of Light.

been a further enlargement in 1805, adding a fine new gallery to accommodate George III's large family. Ironically, it had been completed only just before the old King visited Kew for the last time, and would be used only on exceptional occasions for its original purpose. King George IV had also given a peace offering of an organ which had been built originally for the Castellated Palace. This had been mounted in the east end of the church.

The need now, though, was for space for the villagers themselves. William commissioned Wyatville to extend the church further to the west, increasing the seating by another 200 places. These, he decreed, should be free of pew rents, and he set aside £5,000 to cover the total cost.

Although William would die before this last improvement was completed, the village expressed their thanks in good time. On his next visit in 1836 he was greeted in terms rare for any of the Hanoverian kings, an archway proclaiming in Old Testament language: 'What the King did pleased all the People'.

The Eccentrics of St Anne's

With the death of William IV, Kew lost its last major royal benefactor. As daughter of Edward, Duke of Kent, Queen Victoria owed her crown—indeed her very existence—to her parents' bizarre wedding in Kew Palace in 1818, but she had been brought up in London, and throughout her long reign she would come to Kew only occasionally, and then just to picnic by the Queen's Cottage.

On her accession, one of her 'wicked uncles' immediately left Kew, and another returned. This was because the Kingdom of Hanover was subject to Salic Law under which no woman could succeed. The inheritance passed automatically to the next male heir—the unloved Duke of Cumberland. At the same time, his younger brother, the Duke of Cambridge, who for 20 years had been a a popular Governor-General there, now returned to settle in no. 37 Kew Green, which was renamed Cambridge Cottage.

Cambridge and his family liked Kew and, when they were offered a house in Richmond Park, the Duchess turned it down on the memorable grounds that she preferred Kew Green, as it 'was enlivened by the constant passage of buses to and fro'. The buses then were horse-drawn and certainly did not pass her house—nor was she ever likely to travel in anything so plebeian—but the remark was in keeping with the family's reputation for being approachable and down to earth. This was especially so with Cambridge's massive but ebullient daughter, Mary Adelaide, who became very popular in Kew and Richmond.

The only villagers who were, understandably, less enthusiastic about the Cambridges were the clergy, whose services were punctuated by loud interjections from the eccentric Duke. It might have been less distracting if he had sat in the royal gallery, but he had become very deaf and insisted on sitting in the front row. 'Let us pray,' said the vicar. 'By all

83 Cambridge Cottage, with its distinctive *porte-cochère*—from a 19th-century print.

means,' bawled the Duke. Then to a prayer for rain, the Duke would respond, 'Amen, but you won't get it till the wind changes.'

One curate was so embarrassed by having to compete with the royal running commentary that he resigned, but at that time some of the Kew clergy were almost as eccentric themselves. The Reverend Caleb Colton, for instance, was famous chiefly for spending most of his time in London gambling dens, and living in Soho so as not to have to keep up a house in Kew and the character of a clergyman. Colton, a well known and much quoted wit, was probably thinking of Kew when he coined the saying: 'If you would be known, and not know, vegetate in a village; if you would know and not be known, live in a city.' However, he did appreciate the pulpit in Kew: it was of exactly the right humidity for storing his cigars. He eventually expanded his gambling activities to France and America, lost his living and blew out his brains in Fontainebleau—thereby establishing the first link with Richmond's twin town!

The Other Gardens

In the early 1800s the houses around Kew Green and the hamlet of West Hall could hardly have presented greater contrasts. Kew Green was a fashionable village. There were still a few fishermen there, but most of the population depended on employment in or around its smart houses. Certainly there were a few poor folk, but on the whole they could be coped with via the workhouse and the new school.

On the West Hall/Brick Farm estate, however, life was totally different. Here there were the owners, the Taylors, in their big house, with well-off tenants in West Hall and in the two other houses in the hamlet, West Farm and West Lodge. Otherwise there were no big houses. This was a farming community, and a ruthless one as well.

The men who organised this business were recognised as master market gardeners. They rented

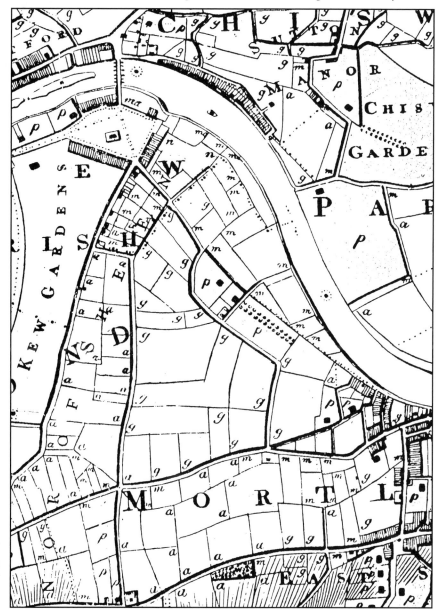

84 Thomas Milne's Land Use Map of 1800.
Key: a. arable; g. market gardens; m. meadow or pasture; n. nursery garden; p. paddock or little park

the land from the landowners—in this case the Taylors—and worked it with itinerant labour, housed in barns or temporary shacks around the estate. When there was no work the labour force moved on.

In the early 1800s the best known of the market gardeners were the Gilpins, the Biggs, and the Graysons. Mr. Grayson not only rented 150 acres from the Taylors; he also had Brick Stables, the farm at the back of West Hall. Mr. Grayson was famous for his asparagus. In 1832 *The Gentleman's Magazine* reported that a bundle of asparagus that had 110 heads and weighed 29lbs had been presented to the Duchess of Bedford by Mr. Grayson, 'the very extraordinary cultivator of asparagus at Mortlake who has repeatedly been awarded distinguished honours by the Royal Horticultural Society for his delicious luxury'.

Wisely the article did not explain why or how the extraordinary Mr. Grayson grew his delicious luxury. Grayson specialised in asparagus because it was ten times as profitable as corn, and the method he used—as did the other market gardeners—was to grow it on London's own sewage. The soil beside the Thames was not particularly rich and the intensive farming of vegetables required constant renewal of the soil. As a result, the vegetables were not so much grown in the soil of Kew and

85 Richard Atwood—the first of the market gardening Atwoods to live in Leyborne Lodge.

86 Pink's Farm—a 1930s photo of the farm once occupied by William Atwood. His farm is now the site of Kew Crematorium.

87   Leyborne Lodge today, still owned by the Atwoods.

Mortlake as in layers of dung that the gardeners spread on top of it, the dung being brought nightly up river from the City to a dock built two hundred yards from the hamlet of West Hall—just where now there is the local sewage works.

Grayson was a cantankerous character. Most of the market gardeners disliked contributing to any improvement in public services, but Grayson took objection to extremes. There was at the time a notorious open sewer, called the Black Ditch, which ran along the line of the Lower Richmond Road. There was a move to have it covered over. Grayson refused to contribute. Fate caught up with him. Coming home late at night he fell into the ditch and drowned. The effect on his family was disastrous. Within a year their business had collapsed and they were working as labourers. They had no land for security as, like most of the market gardeners, Grayson had rented his fields, not owned them.

The chief threat then to the market gardeners along both sides of the Thames was that of competition, especially from abroad. To argue their case they formed a Market Gardeners Association, and elected as secretary and spokesman another well-known gardener from the estate. This was William Atwood, whose family would play a major rôle in the estate for the next hundred years, and whose descendants still live in the house first occupied by William's eldest son, Richard.

Now called Leyborne Lodge, this house was then part of what was generally described as the Brick Farm estate. Richard's brother, William, a pillar of the Mortlake Vestry, lived at the opposite end of the estate at Pink's Farm.

The Atwoods, along with the Dancers, the Pouparts, the Pococks and the Bessants (Grayson's successors), were to be the main market gardeners on the estate for the rest of the 19th century, growing mostly celery, peas, rhubarb, radishes and liquorice, in addition to the money-spinning asparagus. They would all survive the threat of foreign competition, but they would face even bigger problems in the years ahead.

The Artist and the Photographer

For Kew, the almost total departure of royalty could have been a disaster. The court and its courtiers had been the major source of employment. Yet the collapse of this industry seems to have caused little distress, partly because Kew Gardens were now attracting even larger crowds: visitors were admitted daily, except on Sundays, from 1pm to 6pm, free of charge—so long as they were respectably dressed.

However, not everyone was pleased. Though the Gardens were still popular, visitors began to remark that they were beginning to look neglected, and botanists criticised the management. At a parliamentary enquiry in 1838 the supervisor, William Townsend Aiton, son of the first manager of the botanic garden, and himself a distinguished botanist, was castigated for his failure to label plants

88 Lithograph of *Strelitzia Reginae* by Francis Bauer. This plant was named after Queen Charlotte.

89 St Anne's in 1850.

in Kew and for his meanness in distributing them. He complained that he had too little money to do the job properly. Then, to add to the general dismay, the botanical artist, Francis Bauer—the one man at Kew with an international reputation—died in 1840.

Francis Bauer lived in Kew for most of his life, first at 356 Kew Road and then at Eglantine Cottage at the east end of the Green. By birth he was a German, and had been persuaded to settle in Kew by Joseph Banks. He is still seen as one of the great botanical artists of all time; many experts would say the greatest. He is also well known for having played a key rôle in a fascinating controversy outside his chosen field of work.

In 1826, a French friend of Bauer, Nicephore Niepce, who was experimenting with a process later to be known as photography, obtained what is believed to be the first permanent photograph. He called the process Heliography. Finding little support in his own country, Niepce came to stay with Bauer in Kew. Bauer, in recognition of his pre-eminence in his own field, had been elected Secretary of the Royal Society, and was hopeful that the country that had given him such support would do the same for his talented friend. He tried to persuade the Royal Society to back his friend's experiments but, as Niepce refused to divulge the details of his process, the Royal Society rejected the approach.

There are stories of lost images of St Anne's captured by Niepce on pewter. It seems quite likely that he did produce some, but none survives. All that Kew has left from that abortive visit is a Niepce grave in St Anne's churchyard, but this is of the photographer's brother. Niepce himself returned to France, and teamed up with Daguerre, to pioneer the Daguerrotype, and Britain had to wait for Fox Talbot before making its own mark in the history of photography.

79

The Dillman Heritage

Just as Kew, through Francis Bauer, became a mecca for botanical artists, at the same time it established a reputation as the home of another form of art—that of miniature painting. In one way, this was hardly surprising. As Kew Gardens were a natural focus for those who painted flowers, so were royalty an attraction for those who painted portraits. It was for this reason that Meyer came to Kew, where he was appointed Miniature Painter to the King. In contrast his successor in this post was born in Kew. This was George Engleheart, one of the remarkable family of artists descended from Anne Dillman and Thomas Dawney.

Their elder daughter married Francis Engleheart, who may well have been related to the Dillmans. He had come from Germany at the age of 14, been apprenticed to a decorative plasterer and settled in Kew. Although George, a pupil of Sir Joshua Reynolds, was the most distinguished of his sons, all of them were artists or craftsmen. Two were plasterers, one a sculptor, one a builder. All inherited property, either from their father, their mother or from great-uncle John Dillman.

90 John Dillman Engleheart—a miniature by his son, John Cox Engleheart.

91 John Cox Engleheart—a copy made by John Cox Engleheart of a miniature by his uncle, George Engleheart.

92 George Engleheart—a miniature self portrait.

Family Tree of the Englehearts and Richmonds

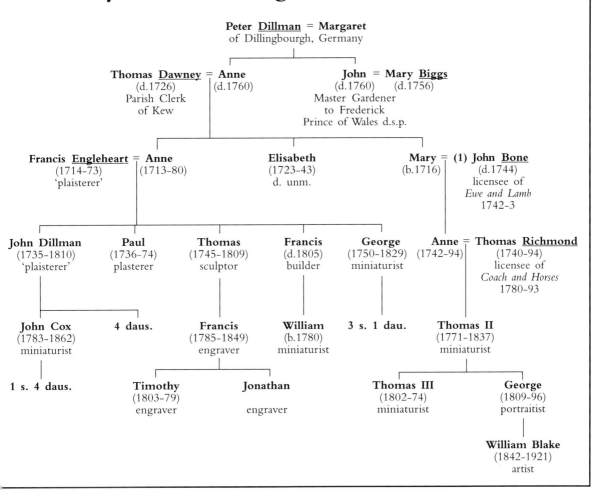

Peter **Dillman** = Margaret
of Dillingbourgh, Germany

Thomas **Dawney** = Anne
(d.1726) (d.1760)
Parish Clerk
of Kew

John = Mary **Biggs**
(d.1760) (d.1756)
Master Gardener
to Frederick
Prince of Wales d.s.p.

Francis **Engleheart** = Anne
(1714–73) (1713–80)
'plaisterer'

Elisabeth
(1723–43)
d. unm.

Mary = (1) John **Bone**
(b.1716) (d.1744)
licensee of
Ewe and Lamb
1742–3

John Dillman
(1735–1810)
'plaisterer'

Paul
(1736–74)
plasterer

Thomas
(1745–1809)
sculptor

Francis
(d.1805)
builder

George
(1750–1829)
miniaturist

Anne = Thomas **Richmond**
(1742–94) (1740–94)
licensee of
Coach and Horses
1780–93

John Cox
(1783–1862)
miniaturist

4 daus.

Francis
(1785–1849)
engraver

William
(b.1780)
miniaturist

3 s. 1 dau.

Thomas II
(1771–1837)
miniaturist

1 s. 4 daus.

Timothy
(1803–79)
engraver

Jonathan
engraver

Thomas III
(1802–74)
miniaturist

George
(1809–96)
portraitist

William Blake
(1842–1921)
artist

The eldest brother, John Dillman Engleheart, received most of the Dillman estate, and then married the heiress to the Middleton land around Mortlake Terrace, with the result that his property in Kew eventually covered nearly all the ground lying within what are now the Kew Road, Broomfield Road, Cumberland Road, and Gloucester Road. The other brothers left Kew, but he stayed on to become a key figure in most of the decisions taken by the Vestry for some thirty years. He also built most of the houses at the end of the Mortlake and Kew Roads closest to the Green.

It is uncertain where he himself lived. He could have lived for a time in Denmark House, or even the biggest house on the whole estate, Gloucester House. This was leased for some years to George III's brother, William Duke of Gloucester, a man whose impact on the village seems to have been limited to giving the house its name. The house itself was left to John Dillman Engleheart's daughter.

His son John Cox, who inherited most of the remaining property, also developed a talent for miniature painting that rivalled that of his uncle. Between them they left, besides some thousands of miniatures of the rich and famous, a unique portrait gallery of their succesful family.

Meanwhile, an equally successful dynasty had descended from Anne Dillman's other daughter, Mary. Mary married a local publican, and so did her daughter, whose husband had been originally the Duke of Gloucester's groom. (Like an earlier settler further down the Kew Road, he had come from Yorkshire, and his name too was Richmond!) From this unlikely strain came four artists: Thomas Richmond, who studied under his cousin George, and was also employed by the royal family; his sons Thomas and George, and finally his grandson, the splendidly named Sir William Blake Richmond. All of the Richmonds were both talented and fashionable, but their talents took them away from Kew.

Many of their ancestors are still there, however, as are John Dillman and several of the Englehearts. They are buried in the churchyard of the parish where, like many of those around them, they were quite rightly honoured, not so much for their national fame, as for their less glamorous but equally exacting work on the local Vestry.

93 No.77 Kew Green. Owned originally by John Dillman, and left to his niece, Anne Engleheart, this has, like no.21 (her other house), fine ceilings, the work either of her husband, Francis Engleheart, or of her son, John Dillman Engleheart.

94 No.358 Kew Road (Denmark House). Nos.356 and 358 Kew Road were once a single house, belonging to the Englehearts. It is likely that the ceilings, though different in style from those of 21 and 77 Kew Green, were by a member of the family.

95 Gloucester House, now the site of Gloucester Court, and once the summer residence of George III's brother, was owned by the Englehearts, and run for many years as a girls' school.

Hooker to the Rescue

Bauer's death in 1840 brought to an end a heated debate over the future of the botanic garden. For two years the government had dithered over what to do. The three wise men it had asked to inspect the garden had recommended that it be expanded and put under new management. The counter argument was that it should be closed and its plants be dispersed. Fortunately the pressure from the scientists proved so great that the government could not take the cheaper option. The Queen agreed to hand over the garden, and the government sent for Sir William Hooker to become the first Director of Kew Gardens.

Hooker was Professor of Botany at Glasgow, and had been persistently lobbying for control of Kew for the last decade. Now he had the post, the power and the promise of money. The unlucky Aiton, who had had to run the garden for 50 years effectively without any of these, was persuaded to resign.

96 Sir William Hooker, the first Director of Kew Gardens.

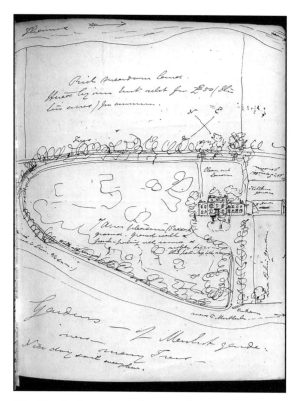

97 West Park—a sketch by Sir William Hooker of the former Brick Farm, his home from 1841 to 1852.

Hooker brought with him to Kew a clear idea of what he wanted to achieve. He also brought a collection of plants and books, so large that it would require 13 rooms of its own. As it was immediately apparent that there was nowhere available round the Green large enough to contain it, Hooker had to look elsewhere for accommodation. He found it in the neighbouring hamlet of West Hall.

It so happened that, just as the Botanic Gardens were changing hands, so were the market gardens down the road. The last of the Taylors had died in 1837 and the estate had passed to yet another cousin, Major-General Leyborne-Popham. This time the beneficiary did not even live nearby. In fact, he probably had never even visited the estate, and would have little time to visit it in the future, for the good reason that he already had a multiplicity of estates

in the West Country, including the magnificent house of Littlecote. Certainly he did not need to use the old house of Brick Farm, where the Taylors had lived. A tenant was needed. Sir William Hooker was exactly what the house required, and the house evidently suited him.

Hooker wrote to his son Joseph, who was at the time one of the scientists on board the *Erebus*, on Ross's Antarctic Expedition:

> Henceforth Kew is my residence & your residence: or rather a very pretty place within ten minutes walk of Kew called *Brick-Farm*. Do not be alarmed at the name:- it may lead you to suppose *Bricks* at some have been made there. No such thing:- except the House is made of *Bricks* & may possibly have been a farm: I know of nothing to justify the name.
>
> The house is plain, but perfectly gentlemanly, ample for all of us (54 windows) with a nice garden & Coach House & Stables, & orchard & paddock & about 7 acres in a nice park-like fence with beautiful & really noble trees. I have besides a noble piece of meadow-land of 10 acres which I let off for £50 a year. All this too is completely in the country, yet from Kew bridge we have Coaches or Omnibuses every quarter of an hour to London for a shilling ...

The only thing he apparently did not like was the name: he changed it to West Park. Joseph, however, did not like the house itself, largely because of its location. Years later he recalled the 'weary walk from our house to the church, all in the mud for Mamma, the want of any neighbour who can come and spend an evening hour with my sister, and my own midnight trudges from the omnibus.'

Obviously West Hall was a lonely hamlet, and one can sympathise with Joseph. Although West Hall was then rented by George Tyrrell, the most ebullient of those picnicking Tyrrell brothers, his wife had just died, and the Graysons were not ideal company for the delicate Mary Hooker.

Hooker's Innovations

Hooker's impact on Kew Gardens was immediately apparent to everyone, botanist and sightseer alike, as his first move was to increase the size of the botanic garden. In its first 80 years it had grown only from nine to eleven acres. Now Hooker asked for another 17 acres. To his delight, the Queen, at the prompting of the Duke of Cambridge, first released 46 acres immediately, and then within the next four years effectively all the old pleasure grounds—with the exception of a few acres, including the Palace and the Cottage.

Hooker welcomed the offer, as the collection increased almost as swiftly as the space, partly because he restored good relations with other botanical collections. Rather than guarding jealously what Kew had collected, he dispersed cuttings and seeds with a generous hand, and naturally benefited from payment in kind. He also shrewdly kept a close eye on his relations with the Government, well aware that it was now his paymaster. It had asked for reports on the use of the garden by the public, and he was determined to prove the popularity of his regime. So he relaxed the conditions under which people might study the plants, and immediately saw a dramatic increase in visitors. In 1841: 9,174; in 1844: 15,114; in 1845: 28,139.

It was not, however, just the plants that attracted them. They found that the gardens were landscaped with their interests in mind. New vistas were created to the Pagoda and to Syon, and a Broad Walk created towards the Palace. The most striking of the changes were, however, in the buildings Hooker commissioned. Within his first ten years the Orangery was redesigned, the main gates completed, innumerable glass houses renovated or replaced and, above all, of course, a brand new Palm House built.

The site chosen for this unique building was picturesque, but potentially troublesome. It was sited where Augusta had had her lake. This lake had been mostly filled in in 1812, leaving just the small stretch of water that now fronts the Palm House, but the ground was still liable to flooding. This would cause some problems, but overall the project was a resounding success. To design the new building, Hooker chose Decimus Burton, the architect of the new main gates. The engineer was William Turner. The botanical experts were Hooker and his new curator, John Smith, a remarkable

98   The Palm House, designed by Burton, and opened in 1848.

99 The Main Gates today.

gardener whom Hooker had promoted on taking over the gardens. All members of this directing team deserve credit for the beautiful, and practical, building, and most especially for sinking their considerable differences of opinion for the greater good of the project.

At the end of the decade, the royal family made two more gifts to the Gardens, both very welcome though one of them less generous than it appeared. They handed over two houses: Metholds House (Hell House, since rebuilt, and named after its most recent tenant, a wine merchant), and Hunter House. Hooker could now move closer to the Gardens. He and his family moved into Metholds House, which has ever since been known as the Director's House, and he moved his collection into Hunter House where it became the nucleus of today's Herbarium.

The history of Hunter House was an odd one. In 1818, it had been bought by the Crown, and there had been tentative plans for using it even then as a herbarium. Nothing happened however and it had for some years been used by the King of Hanover when in England, at which time it was called Hanover House. Now he had died and it was at last to be used by the Gardens. Everyone naturally thanked the Queen profusely—no one at the time being aware that Hunter House was not hers to give. George IV had already sold it to the Government back in 1823 to help to pay his debts; he had then pocketed the money and never handed it over!

Theft at St Anne's

In 1845 Kew's church fell prey to yet another of what were becoming a chronic series of crises. The church registers were stolen. In itself that was no great disaster. Most churches have gaps in their records, and some can trace these to bizarre thefts—people do occasionally have reasons for hiding the truth of their paternity or age—but the St Anne's theft was more bizarre than most. The Armada chest in which the registers were kept was stolen. There was a—somewhat muted—hue and cry. Then the chest was recovered. It was found in the Thames, but with all the records missing.

For years no one could discover who had taken the chest or why, but eventually the Taylor family owned up to the theft. One of the longest established families in the village, the Taylors were of some interest in themselves. In the mid-1700s they were well off; then they lost most of their money. To survive, they became the village bakers. Even as bakers, however, at least once the Taylors had to be rescued by the Vestry, either because the

100 The Armada Chest. These iron strongboxes, with keyholes and complex bolts in the lids, were imported from the Continent in the 16th and 17th centuries. They had no connection with the Spanish Armada.

SACRILEGE.
TEN GUINEAS REWARD.

WHEREAS the Parish Church of **St. ANNE's, KEW,** was entered on the Night of **SATURDAY,** the **22nd Instant,** and the **IRON CHEST,** CONTAINING THE **Parish Registers** AND OTHER PAPERS STOLEN THEREFROM,

The above Reward will be given to any Person who will give such information as will lead to the conviction of the Offender or Offenders, on application to

EDWARD SCARD, ESQ.

February 24, 1845.   CHURCHWARDEN, KEW.

F. H. WALL, PRINTER, CASTLE TERRACE, RICHMOND.

101   Handbill on the theft of St Anne's registers in 1845.

village could not exist without bread, or because of the friends they had. Certainly it was not an enemy that revealed their rôle in the theft. It was—years later—their own descendants. Apparently the story was passed down the generations that they had been asked to take the registers by certain members of the royal family, and that being fervent royalists they had agreed. The story did not specify which members of the royal family were involved, nor what happened to the registers.

Inevitably people raised the old rumours about George III's marriage to Hannah Lightfoot, but the registers taken were more recent: they covered marriages from 1783 to 1838, baptisms from 1791 to 1845, and burials from 1785 to 1845. What could have been the royal family's interest in these?

Then there were suggestions that perhaps Hannah's son, George Rex, might have married one of the royal princesses at St Anne's and that was why he was sent abroad so summarily. The truth will probably never be known. Certainly the Taylor family know no more.

However, the incident seems by chance to have blighted the life of George Rex's daughter. She had married a Reverend Charles Bull. In the late 1840s Bull came to England and asked St Anne's if he could see their registers—a tactless question in view of the recent theft. First, someone broke into Bull's lodgings and burned his papers. Then he was hastily posted off as chaplain to the Falkland Islands for 15 years.

It is uncertain why his enquiry should have caused such concern, but in the 1840s Victoria was still an untried monarch, and a Mrs. Ryves was pursuing a case to prove that she was legitimately descended from George III's brother. As her case rested on documents that indicated that the Reverend Dr. Wilmot had married both brothers, as described on page 41, it was clear that if she were right then the Rex family too were of legitimate royal birth. Though the judiciary managed to postpone the hearing of her case for some 20 years, before rejecting her claim in 1866, perhaps those in power were nervous. They would have seen her evidence and might have been worried.

It looked impressive then, and it still does. Only recently released for public view, it will soon be stored in the new Public Record Office building in Kew, ironically only a few hundred yards from where just possibly the ceremony itself took place.

Before Mrs. Ryves was finally permitted to fight, and lose, her case to be recognised a princess, the last of the established royals to live on in Kew had had their own domestic dramas.

In 1850 the Duke of Cambridge died at Cambridge Cottage. His funeral was suitably ornate, but he had chosen as his resting place his own parish church of St Anne's. The next year his son, who was to become one of the longest serving, and most reactionary, of British Commanders-in-Chief, erected a little mausoleum for the family at the east end of the church.

In the 1930s the royal remains were taken to Windsor to join their relations in Frogmore Mausoleum, and the Kew mausoleum is now used for the ashes of parishioners, but there are still mementos in the church of those of the Royal Family that died within the village. At the time royal deaths were marked by hanging hatchments as a sign of mourning outside the house. These diamond-shaped boards displayed the arms of the deceased. Later they were stored within the church. Although St Anne's hatchments have now been dispersed for safe keeping, copies can still be seen on the royal gallery.

More happily, and to everyone's delighted surprise, in 1866 the large and lovable Princess Mary Adelaide of Cambridge not only became engaged in Kew but also married there. For the first event she, or her fiancé His Serene Highness the Duke of Teck, chose the Rhododendron Dell. For the second, she chose St Anne's. Her contemporary, and recently widowed, cousin the Queen turned up in deepest black, but it was nevertheless the biggest and most important wedding the little church had ever seen. No doubt Edward, Prince of Wales, enlivened the proceedings, as he was very fond of his Cambridge cousins. When confined with his tutors at White Lodge in Richmond Park, he used to escape in the evenings and row himself down river to Kew to dine at Cambridge Cottage.

Ironically, May, the eldest child of this unexpected marriage, would in time herself become engaged to both of Edward's sons. The first would die before the wedding, but as the wife of the second son, George V, she would herself return many times to her grandparents' village as Queen Mary.

102　The Royal Gallery with copies of the royal hatchments.

103　Queen Victoria and Prince Edward at the wedding of her cousin Mary Adelaide of Teck in St Anne's in 1866.

Joseph Hooker Succeeds

1865 saw the opening of the second great building of Sir William Hooker's directorship, the Temperate House. Designed by Burton, it required so much gravel for its terraces that a huge hole was created beside the Syon vista. Making a virtue out of what could have been an eyesore, the architects created a lake. This immediately became in itself one of the Gardens' great attractions, as did the flagpole, which was raised in 1859. Flagpoles have limited life and the present one is the fourth to be given to the Gardens, each one being a little longer than its predecessors. All of them of them have come from British Columbia.

The Temperate House provided, amongst other purposes, a new home for the contents of Kew's first stove, built by Chambers in 1761, which had long needed replacing. Its site, marked by a metal frame covered with wisteria, is now appropriately overlooked by the Princess of Wales Conservatory, named after Augusta.

Sir William Hooker himself died in 1865. He had done so much for the Gardens that the country might well have assumed that this was the equivalent of a national disaster. Who could possibly succeed him? In fact, there was never any doubt over who would be appointed, nor over what would then happen. Sir William had already ensured that his son Joseph would succeed, confident that he would follow his father's vision, and that he would follow it even more effectively.

Sir William's fond expectations were in the event justified. Joseph was not just groomed for the job; he was even better qualified than his father had been. He was a brilliant scientist. (A close friend of Darwin and Huxley, he would be elected President of the Royal Society, and eventually receive the Order of Merit.) He had also proved himself possibly the greatest of all plant collectors. He would direct the Gardens with authority and imagination. However, his style was noticeably different from his father's. Where William was a diplomat, prepared to spend hours mollifying sensitive scientists and difficult dukes, Joseph took all problems head-on. He was by nature combative.

Joseph made a characteristically distinctive contribution to the scientific work of the gardens, by commissioning the first Jodrell Laboratory in 1876 and an extension to the Herbarium in 1877. No less characteristic though were the public battles he fought against government ministers who dared to interfere in the work of the Gardens, and against members of the general public who suggested a more liberal approach to opening hours.

104 The Temperate House.

105 The Victorian press reaction to the campaign for longer opening hours at Kew Gardens—and for the lowering of 'that unsightly wall'.

He was especially rigid when faced by local pressure groups. When Richmond Vestry had asked William Hooker to lower the high wall along the Kew Road and top it with railings—as was the custom with public gardens in London—he had simply advised the Ministry that it could not be done. When they repeated the request in 1877, Joseph's response was characteristically robust. He told the Minister that 'the damage to the vegetation would be incalculable'. Rather than lower it, they must *add* at least two feet, he wrote, 'to stop the workmen climbing over...'

There was no money in the budget for this addition, and it is hard to imagine any workmen fighting to get at Sir Joseph's plants. Still, rather than face the Director's wrath, the civil servants somehow found the money to do what he demanded. Then further protests caused the Ministry to waver. Sir Joseph was made of sterner stuff. 'If you stop now the residents will regard it as due to the remonstrances,' he wrote. The work resumed.

Sir Joseph was particularly sensitive at the time, as he was under pressure to extend the opening hours. People wanted the Gardens open in the mornings. In 1878 this campaign reached its height with cartoons in the press, and allegations that the Gardens had become 'a sort of happy hunting ground for the scientifically inclined members of the Hooker family'. Sir Joseph refused to give way, won his point in principle, but then was wise enough to concede an hour. The opening was moved to 12 noon. That was as far as Sir Joseph would go.

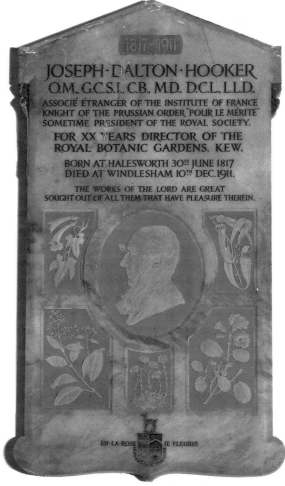

106 The memorial to Sir Joseph Hooker in St Anne's.

The Railway reaches Kew

The most significant event during the reign of Joseph Hooker at Kew was something not of his making, yet with which he was very much concerned. In 1869 the railway came to Kew.

Of course, its arrival had been a subject of thought, planning and correspondence—Sir Joseph was an assiduous writer. He knew that visitors were vital. He might object to the common man and woman interrupting the work of his gardeners, but he was well aware that without their enthusiasm there might be cuts in the Government's budget for his scientific work.

For him, as for the rest of Kew, the key date was 1868 when Kew railway bridge was due to be completed—to carry first the London and South Western Railway, then the District Line, through Kew to Richmond.

He and his staff had decided that the ideal approach to the Gardens was direct from the new line down towards the Temperate House. With this in mind, he had exceptionally allowed for a lowering of the wall where there could be a new gate. All that was needed was a confirmation from the board of the London and South Western Railway that the Kew station would be at the end of an avenue leading to the Temperate House.

Then, presumably because they needed more space for their sidings, the LSWR decided that the Kew station would not be opposite the Temperate House, but some six hundred yards to the north.

For the Gardens it must have been very irritating. It would not affect the numbers of visitors, but it deprived them of the dramatic

107 Kew Road in 1912. Seven shops and cottages (nos.320-332) were removed by the 1917 widening of the Kew Road. Mr. Twinn's greengrocer's shop survives as part of no.318. Mr. James's refreshment rooms and the cottages gave way to the present entrance to Gloucester Court. James's name survives: it is attached to the cottages farther down the road.

108 Newens Refreshment Rooms. Now known as The Maids of Honour Restaurant—the recipe for the famous tarts is still strictly guarded by the family—this is the most famous of all Kew's tea houses. The shop is now run by Peter and John Newens, son and grandson of the boy holding the pony.

entrance they expected. In the event both railway and Gardens would reach a happy compromise, but for the interim what should be done with the gap in the wall? Joseph Hooker might have been known for his implacable opposition to gaps in the wall, and for his disdain for public pressure, but on this one occasion, when the public demanded that the roadside view of the Temperate House be retained, he conceded the point. The gap was left, and it remains to this day.

It was perhaps less surprising an outcome than it seemed at the time. After all, the original gap in the wall was made by the Gardens. They had learned to live with it. To fill it in would have been in its way an admission of failure over the siting of the station. If the LSWR was stupid enough to change its mind, the same should not

be said of the Gardens. They had taken their decision and would stay with it.

Meanwhile the government could be placated by the figures the Director was able to report. Through the 1870s the numbers of visitors increased rapidly, until by 1883 he was able to announce an attendance figure of 1,244,161.

Sir Joseph—he had been knighted in 1877—retired in 1885, far earlier than expected, as his doctors had given him only two years to live. With a characteristic refusal to bow to the opinions of others, he survived as energetic as ever to 1911. By then he was 94. The family was offered a funeral and burial at Westminster Abbey, but Sir Joseph remained uncooperative to the last. He had already decided where he was to be buried: beside his father at St Anne's—a Kewite to the last.

The Opening of the Cumberland Gate

The arrival of the railway in Kew not only brought the world to see the Gardens in numbers that would have been quite inconceivable a few years before; it fundamentally changed the village. Just as the courtiers in Tudor times built houses in Kew because they had discovered it on their way to pay court to the King at Richmond, so now commuters who had come to see the Gardens stayed on to buy houses for themselves.

Both the Selwyns and the Englehearts had anticipated this reaction, and houses were already being built on both estates ready to attract this custom. Eventually both would benefit equally from the influx, but for the first few years they would compete for custom. At first it seemed that the Selwyns had the edge, with their plans to build an avenue from the station to the Temperate House.

109 352 Kew Road, once home of Walter Deverell.

With the change of station site, however, the Englehearts seized their chance.

In the 1860s nearly all the property originally owned by John Dillman Engleheart was held by his grandson, John Gardner Dillman Engleheart. Some of it already contained housing, which had been built to accommodate the gradual expansion of the village over the last hundred years. There were also a few houses down the south side of Mortlake Road, and a far longer line of houses and cottages spreading up the east side of Kew Road.

Engleheart reacted quickly to the news that Kew Gardens station was to be placed on what was then the edge of the Leyborne-Popham market gardens. The nearest road—in fact the only road anywhere near the station—was Sandy (Sandy-combe) Lane, which in those days incorporated Broomfield Road. For visitors it would be the only approach to the Gardens from the station, but it was hardly ideal as there was no entrance to the Gardens where it met the Kew Road.

There was, however, a small entrance a little to the north, surmounted by the lion from George IV's abortive gate across Kew Green. This entrance was almost opposite the *Cumberland Arms* on the Engleheart estate. Engleheart proposed to the Gardens that the entrance be widened, and given an appropriately impressive gate. He would pay the bills. What was more, he would build at his own expense a new road, to be called Kew Gardens Road, connecting the new gate to the station.

This might not match Hooker's original vision of a straight avenue direct from the station to the Temperate House, but at least it was practical and would cost the Gardens nothing. It was too good an offer to reject. So the lion was once more sent on its travels, now down to the far end of the Gardens wall, where it still presides over the pedestrian entrance next to the Queen's Gate. Meanwhile Engleheart was given gracious permission to build what would be called Cumberland Gate.

Engleheart could now push ahead with plans he had been refining over the previous two years. Gloucester Road had been established some years before, and was now steadily built up. (By 1876 they had reached no. 23; by 1882, no. 66 was occupied.) At the same time, slightly larger houses were built all the way up Kew Gardens Road, which was linked to the Mortlake Road by another two lines of houses bordering Cumberland Road.

The use of Cumberland in the names of the gate and the road—and indeed the naming of Cumberland Place and Hanover Place in Kew Road—marked what had once been a close connection between the estate and the Dukes of Cumberland. (For decades the Cumberlands had leased the Engleheart property beside the *Coach and Horses*, around what became Bank House.) Consequently, the most unpopular of the royal dukes is ironically the one most widely commemorated in Kew.

110 *The Pet* by Walter Deverell. This picture, now in the Tate, is one of the few left by this talented Pre-Raphaelite, and includes a clear view of the Victorian garden of no.352.

While Kew took its first faltering steps into the modern world of the commuter, there was a late flowering of artistic interest in the village, which recalled the days of Gainsborough and Zoffany.

These 19th-century artists, however, were very different from their distinguished predecessors. They did not come in pursuit of patronage. They came mostly in search of peace and privacy. Nor were they friends and colleagues. Two were Pre-Raphaelites, but the others pursued widely differing artistic aims and lifestyles. Indeed, although four of them were close contemporaries, it is doubtful if they met each other in Kew, or would have found anything in common if they had. It was the place rather than the people that seems to have attracted them.

Walter Deverell (1827-54) was one of those sad figures in the world of art, known more for the rich promise of their imagination than for the pictures they left behind. Deverell died young of Bright's disease. For several years he lived in no. 352 Kew Road, then called Heathfield House, and he had a studio at the end of the garden where now there are garages. It is said that Dante Gabriel Rossetti used to work there too, both of them painting Mary Siddall. Certainly Deverell discovered Mary as a model, but no works of his survive with her in them, and the only painting we can confidently ascribe to his time in Heathfield is *The Pet*, the setting of which is clearly recognisable in the garden behind the 18th-century house.

Arthur Hughes (1832-1915), now far better known than Deverell, did not move to Kew till after Deverell's death. He bought Eastside House (no. 22 Kew Green) in 1858. Among the Pre-Raphaelites he was loved for his gentle and easy-going disposition, but at the time his work was less marketable than most, hovering as it did on the knife edge between sentiment and sentimentality. He brought up his family in Kew, many of them appearing in his pictures.

As he wrote to a friend, 'My painting room is a very nice little one, but it is at the far end of my garden and while unwell it is far indeed...' Despite illness, however, Hughes outlived nearly all his Pre-Raphaelite contemporaries, and painted vigorously to the end of his life.

Marianne North (1830-90) never lived in Kew, but is associated with it in a way that no other painter is. She not only left the Gardens her collection of flower paintings, but also built for them the gallery named after her near the Temperate House. She was one of a number of ladies whose travels give the lie to the conventional picture of cosseted Victorian womenfolk. She was also a talented and influential botanic artist in her own right, bringing back to Britain pictures of flowers that until then were unknown even to the Kew botanists.

Camille Pissarro (1830-1903) came to Kew in very different circumstances. Kew had a reputation for attracting artists from abroad, but the arrival of the father of French Impressionism in 1892 was unexpected and largely unrecognised. He had come to Kew to try to sort out a domestic difficulty. His son Lucien was living in England and had fallen in love with a Jewess, whose parents were set against the match. After long discussions with Camille they reluctantly allowed the wedding to go ahead. Meanwhile Camille painted scenes in Kew, most of them now in private hands. At the time he was staying on Kew Green at the corner of Gloucester Road, scarcely twenty yards away from his exact contemporary, Arthur Hughes. In character the two elderly artists were very much

112 *The Californian Dogwood* by Marianne North.

114 *The Pagoda* by James Lewis. Though the Pagoda must have been an obvious subject for a pub painter such as Lewis, few Lewis pictures of it survive. Perhaps—even then—the entry charge was too high for him!

alike, but in any discussion on art they are unlikely to have had much in common.

James Lewis (1861-1934) was a pub artist who painted for his supper—in his case mostly liquid. For many years his paintings decorated the walls of the local pubs in Kew and Richmond, where they had been left in settlement of his bar bills. Many others were commissioned on the spot from Lewis as attractive wedding presents. Now most are in private hands, often overseas. They were painted on board, on untreated canvas, even on wallpaper—whatever came to hand. Some have consequently suffered. At the time they were seen as cheap and cheerful gifts, and only recently has Lewis been recognised as a landscape artist of importance. Recognition, however, came too late. He lies in Richmond cemetery in a pauper's grave.

The Selwyn Estate

While the Engleheart estate eagerly seized its opportunity to become the prime route from the new station to the Gardens, the Selwyns pursued their own developments at a more measured pace.

Although the estates had much in common, in that most of the land in both cases had been used for agriculture, there had been distinct differences in style. Since the 1770s the Englehearts had always been eager to build houses, as and when the demand had spread beyond the Green. Meanwhile the rest of their land was used as meadows, presumably to fatten up 'Welsh Beasties'. In contrast, the Selwyn estate, as we can see from Milne's Land Use Map on p.75, was primarily arable. There had been one or two big houses down the Kew Road, and a few farm workers had lived in the Sandy/Blind Lane (later Victoria) Cottages from the 1830s, but the remaining property was under cultivation.

For centuries, this land had made fair profits from supplying London with cereal crops, though the profits were smaller than those of the market gardeners around West Hall. Then, from the 1840s the Selwyns' tenant farmers' incomes began to fall sharply. With the spread of the railways, food was being brought into London cheaply from far afield. They seem to have switched to market gardening, and then to orchards in an effort to find a product that was still in short supply, but to no avail. The farmers' plight was typical of what was now happening everywhere along the banks of the lower Thames—as the tenants' profits dropped, and they found it harder to pay their rents, the owners were tempted by offers from developers.

The Selwyns were typical too of the owners of such sites. They might live on the property—in their case in the family home of Selwyn Court (formerly Pagoda House)—but they were not themselves farmers. The founder of the estate, Charles Selwyn, had died childless. Deciding that his eldest brother's children—especially the witty but worthless George—neither needed extra estates nor deserved them, he left his estate to William, second son of his younger brother. This Selwyn built Pagoda House, and left the estate to his son, William, who had three sons: his heir the Lord Justice Charles Jasper Selwyn, the Professor of Divinity at Cambridge and the Bishop of Lichfield.

The Lord Justice's sons developed the land, and the family house disappeared without trace in 1895. (It stood approximately where Christchurch is now.)

All that are left of the Selwyns' stewardship of the land are the names they gave the roads. The origin of some of these remains obscure, but most are emphatically familial. Selwyn and Pagoda mark the extent of their own house and gardens. Hatherley and Fitzwilliam were family friends, while Holmesdale, Branstone and Lichfield commemorate respectively an estate, a parish and a bishopric all once in Selwyn hands. The last of these was to be the most significant, as Lichfield Road now provides

KEW from the Air.

the avenue approach to the station that Hooker and the Selwyns had hoped for 30 years before. Even this took its time. Though Lichfield was developed early, it was not until 1889 that the Leyborne-Popham estate agreed that it could be extended across their land to link up with the station.

The most striking feature of this very large development was the difference in size between the biggest and the smallest houses. All along the Kew Road there were large houses, designed for the carriage trade; elsewhere there were more modest homes, while Elizabeth Cottages, a fairly late development, was deliberately designed on the scale of Victoria Cottages.

Some of the smallest houses put up at this time were built on several comparatively small fields that did not belong to the Selwyns at all. They belonged to the Crown, having been outlying paddocks of George III's farm. Two roads, therefore, had royal names—Alexandra and Battenburg. The latter has since then changed its name. In the First World War, when the Battenburgs diplomatically became Mountbattens, the road went further. It changed its name to Windsor. It was to prove prophetic. Many years later Prince Philip, heir to the Mountbatten name, took the same decision.

115 The Growth of the Selwyn Estate. This postcard catches the estate in mid-development, but it must be before 1923 as there are no signs of the Gainsborough Road houses.

99

The Parish of St Luke

The hectic growth in population both within and around London in the 1800s created social problems beyond the experience of those responsible for what then passed for local government. The greatest problem was that few of the new housing estates had centres around which community life could develop.

In Kew, this was particularly the case for those who had come to live on the Selwyn estate. The new householders here were technically within the parish of Richmond, but they tended to gravitate towards Kew because they used Kew Gardens station. They were thus in danger of being disregarded by both Kew and Richmond. As elsewhere, one of the first to try to fill this vacuum was the Church of England. The diocese decided that a new church and a new church school were needed.

As so often in the history of the church, the site was provided free. In fact two sites were provided free. First the Pouparts—then as now a major name in the making of jam—offered a site on the edge of their market gardens in Sandy Lane. The Pouparts were one of a number of Huguenot families that had set up as market gardeners along the Thames. Unlike many of their rivals—perhaps because of their background—they coped well with new developments: they were prepared to move whenever push came to shove. So, as developers outbid the prices the market gardeners were prepared to pay, they moved steadily further west along the Thames. By 1876 they had already moved twice, first from Bermondsey to Battersea, and then on to Mortlake. William Poupart was farming a huge spread of fields in the neighbourhood, and had even bought some of the land along Sandy Lane. He now generously offered a site on its west side to the diocese.

The diocese eagerly accepted the offer. They built an 'iron church' with a small schoolroom attached. Both would be named after St Luke. Almost immediately, however, it became clear that the site and the building were far too small. Fortunately, the Selwyns were now happy to contribute land as well. So in 1888 a new church

116 The Initial Plan for St Luke's. This design for the church indicates a spire that was never realised. In the 1980s it acquired a small tower, built to accommodate a lift.

was built on their land, alongside the avenue that led to the Temperate House. This was designed on elaborate lines, on the assumption that the new parish would be catering for hundreds every Sunday.

At the same time the diocese moved the old iron building over to the other side of the road, and built a proper school, ironically on far less generous lines than the church. It was a miscalculation. The school, excellently directed though it was through the next century, was always to be the poor relation of the bigger Queen's School. The Pouparts' gift, however, has not been wasted. The building lives on as St Luke's House Educational Centre, still contributing vitally to the educational life of the village.

The Doughty Estate

While Engleheart and the Selwyns were developing their estates, new cottages and houses were also beginning to appear on and around Miss Doughty's former land.

On her death, most of her estate had gone to Edward Tichborne, and as such was an element in the great court case when the so-called Tichborne Claimant tried to establish his right to the family inheritance. By then, though, it must have been a very minor element, as by the mid-1800s her large estate had been divided into far smaller ones. The area beside the Green was occupied by Priory Lodge, the substantial house now known as Cecil Lodge. Next there was a smaller house, called the Casino, while Miss Doughty's little Priory itself had been transformed into what was called 'a gentleman's residence', and was overshadowed on the east by the new railway embankment.

The process continued. In 1875 and 1877 the gentleman's residence and its grounds were sold and then sold again. Briefly the Casino grew into Priory Park House. Then that and the Priory disappeared altogether, along with most of the Priory Lodge grounds. The developers had moved in. By 1886 Forest, Maze and Priory roads were on their way.

These new houses were built specifically with commuters in mind. These had come to Kew to escape from the smoke of London and to enjoy the convenience of a railway on the doorstep. Garden space was a feature, but there was little demand for horses and carriages, while the motor car had yet to be developed.

At the same time, down by the riverside a different transformation was taking place. Here there had been no big houses—just meadows, trees and rushes. By 1850, pollution had effectively ended fishing as a trade, but another ancient riverside trade had clung on for a few more years, that of harvesting the osiers (willows) and rushes of the riverbank. For centuries along the riverside and on the aits Kew people had pollarded the willows to make hurdles and baskets from the thicker twigs and sieves from the slender ones. The reeds had been gathered for thatching or covering the floors. Towards the end of the 19th century, however, the demand was waning, and those who

117 The Sale notice of the Priory Estate in 1875, indicating the break-up of Miss Doughty's estate, prior to development.

had been granted riverside land under the Enclosure Acts decided to sell off their land for housing.

Here the developers built cottages, some for the artisans, but others clearly for moneyed people. The first of Westerly Ware's Willow Cottages were built in 1861, followed by Thetis in 1883. Then in 1886 and 1887 first Cambridge and then Watcombe

101

118 *(above)* The last of the fishermen. As late as 1809 there were reports of 'ten or twenty salmon taken at draught', but by 1850 pollution had virtually destroyed this ancient industry.

119 *(left)* Harvesting the willows. The willow trees were regularly pollarded every winter for fencing and hurdles.

Cottages went up. These were on the old Twiggetts meadow, which had had twa' gates, one on either side of the dock. The cottages had charm but they also had a major disadvantage: they were liable to frequent flooding, as the river took revenge for the loss of its ancient trades.

The New Queen's School

Cambridge and Watcombe Cottages were not the only buildings on Twiggetts. They stood either side of the little gothic Queen's School. (Queen Victoria had permitted it to change its name on her accession in 1837.) The school was, in fact, far too little, and had been so for some time. It needed replacing.

If the story of schooling—or rather the lack of it—on Kew Green had been an embarrassment to those responsible in the 18th century, then the village could take pride for managing matters better subsequently.

The first managers, appreciating that demand would soon exceed supply, had wisely bought extra land immediately after the school was first put up in 1824. They were therefore ready to build a larger building so soon as they could be confident of raising the money. Meanwhile they did the best they could in the circumstances.

120   *(right)* The regulations on churchgoing ...

121   ... and extracts from a Queen's School headteacher's log book *(below)*.

Boys and girls were educated separately under a Headmaster and a Headmistress, from the age of five to fourteen. The education was free for the local children; non-residents were charged 2d a day. Money was raised by subscription, and by annual charity sermons. (In the 19th century they took their fundraising seriously!) They were lucky too to have the Capel charity and royal patronage: there was an annual contribution from the Sovereign, and enthusiastic backing from the Cambridge family. Cambridge enthusiasm, however, was not always an advantage as the Duchess, an assiduous visitor, on at least one occasion backed an incompetent teacher against the managers. The Hookers must have sympathised—the Cambridges were for ever telling them how run the Gardens.

From the headteachers' reports it appears to have been a typical Church school of its day, committed to inculcating Christian virtues and a proper sense of the children's position in life—that of service to their 'betters'. The reports have their lighter moments, but their general tone is sombre and occasionally tragic. There are several accounts of children dying, including one of how the headteacher lost two of his own children to diphtheria caught from the insanitary condition of the creek that ran beside the school. The creek was covered over, but it remained a health hazard for years.

Throughout the century the population of the village rose by about 100 each decade, until 1880. Then in one year it shot up by 500. The school was bursting at its seams. Faced by this crisis the managers sensibly decided not just to provide for the current need but to build on the expectation that this rapid increase in population would persist. The latest Duke of Cumberland, whose family had been as generous, if less obtrusive, patrons of the school as their cousins the Cambridges, laid the foundation stone of the new building in 1887.

The new school, unlike its predecessor, had no architectural pretensions, nor was it particularly easy to run—the classrooms were on three storeys—but it was a substantial and spacious building. To the credit of its managers, it would cope adequately not only with the increase in numbers over the next 70 years, but also with the very different expectations of the parents who would send their children there in the 20th century.

122 The school, as rebuilt in 1887.

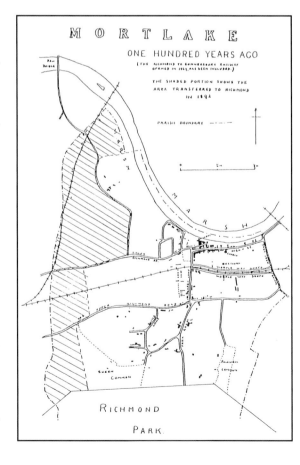

Kew Incorporated

By the 1890s the mushroom growth of Kew and Richmond forced a revolution in the structure of their local government. Richmond—by far the larger of the two—led the way.

In the 18th century, under Charles Selwyn's guidance, Richmond had set an example to the rest of the country as a pioneering local authority, but by the end of the 19th its system was antediluvian compared with some of its neighbours. Its local services were still run by the members of the Vestry, some of whom served ex-officio because of their positions in the parish church, while the others were elected on a severely restricted suffrage. In contrast, all ratepayers in neighbouring Kingston had been able to vote for their representatives since the 1830s.

The Vestrymen were responsible for the maintenance and lighting of highways, the collection of refuse, the supply of water, and the enforcement of building regulations and bye-laws. The critics of the Richmond Vestry argued that, with Parliament being elected by what then passed for universal suffrage, it was indefensible that an unrepresentative body should wield so much power. After a fierce campaign the critics won the day, and in 1890 Richmond was granted incorporation as a borough.

Immediately Richmond made approaches to the Vestries of Kew and Petersham, suggesting that they would gain by becoming part of the wonderful new borough. After considerable debate both villages agreed, and a bill to that effect was presented to Parliament. This, however, was not all that was in the bill. With a minimum of consultation, Richmond also proposed to take over 625 acres of Mortlake parish, including almost all the Leyborne-Popham estate. Mortlake was furious, and pointed out that Richmond would be taking a tenth of their income and assuming only one twenty-fourth of their liabilities. Richmond modified their claims, but still managed to get away with 329 acres of their neighbour's land in what became known as the Rape of North Sheen. As a result, in 1892 Kew parish became Kew Ward in

the Borough of Richmond, while St Luke's and the Richmond part of the Leyborne-Popham estate were incorporated in Richmond North Ward.

There is no evidence that those who lived on the estate objected, and the case put by Mortlake was poorly fought. This may have been partly because there had recently been a grave division within the Mortlake Vestry, in which the Congregationalists had tried in their own way to end the power of the ex-officio Church of England members. The nonconformists were led on that occasion by John Doulton, a distinguished resident of the West Hall hamlet. The Doulton family had their china works by Vauxhall Bridge, and John Doulton lived at West Park. Nonconformity had been a potent force in Mortlake since the days of John Juxon, and it is possible that, even after Doulton's early death, there remained a strong minority that might have preferred being part of Richmond Borough to being ruled by Mortlake Vestry.

The Rape of North Sheen was remarkable not just because it overrode the objections of Mortlake Vestry, but also because it cut off most of the market garden estate from its farm buildings in the hamlet of West Hall. On the other hand it tidied up an anomaly. The parish of Kew had had a strip of meadow that stretched along the riverside some three hundred yards from the railway bridge into Mortlake parish. It was bordered by the Kingston Creek. The new boundary now went straight up from the mouth of the Creek, following the line of Cut-Throat Lane to Gipsy Corner.

Gipsy Corner, for centuries a regular camping ground for gipsies, is of course still there at the end of Kew Meadows Path, but the Creek and the Lane have both long disappeared and, with Mortlake now part of Richmond upon Thames, the boundary they marked is no longer needed. Only on old maps can you find their somewhat misleading names. Certainly there were murders in the market gardens, but not in Cut-Throat Lane. It was the common name give to cut-through alleys. As for Kingston Creek, and the Kingston Bridge that once crossed it on the towpath, they are indeed, though many miles away, named after Kingston, as the Creek marked the boundary of the old Kingston Hundred.

123 *(facing page)* The Rape of North Sheen. The shaded portion on this map, drawn by H. Spears, illustrates the area incorporated by the Richmond Borough in 1892.

The Last of the Royals

With the turn of the century, Kew lost its last close link with the royal family. In 1904, the Duke of Cambridge died and Cambridge Cottage was handed over to the Gardens.

Queen Victoria had by then relinquished the one building for which she had a personal affection, the Queen's Cottage. When she had been younger, she would come and picnic there, as her parents had done on their wedding day. It seemed a suitable gift to mark her Jubilee. The grounds of Kew Palace also went to the Gardens, while the Palace itself was to be a museum to the life and times of George III.

The Director to benefit from these gifts was the last of the Hooker dynasty, Sir William Thistleton-Dyer. He had succeeded to the job, as it were by divine right, having married Sir Joseph's daughter. For the Gardens this was a time for consolidation, rather than innovation, and the new Director was happy to consolidate.

Though a distinguished scientist, Sir William made his mark as an administrator. As such, he was at least as combative as his father-in-law, and considerably more eccentric. He had a passion for uniforms, imposing them on his staff and parading himself whenever possible in his rôle as an Inspector of Constabulary. He was a great disciplinarian. Characteristically, when he was eventually persuaded to employ women gardeners, he insisted that they wear 'brown bloomers, thick woollen stockings and ordinary brown peaked caps'. He was, he said, not going to encourage any 'sweethearting'.

124 Kew Palace. This postcard gives an austere picture of the old Dutch House when first opened to the public. In fact, royal life there, though hardly luxurious, probably suffered from too much rather than too little furniture.

Industrial Breakthrough

Kew Gardens station had made an immediate impact on the Gardens and on the development of houses in Kew. Yet, for its first 15 years, the station itself remained oddly isolated; there was a station buffet there and not much else.

Most of the local shopping then was conducted on the Green, or up and down Sandy Lane (promoted to Sandycombe Road from 1884), where 'on Saturdays people walked on each other's heads', while the few tea houses for those who visited by train were on the Kew Road around the Cumberland Gate.

It was not until the late 1880s that businesses began to spring up around the station, initially in wooden lock-up shops in Station Approach. Appropriately two were estate agents, one of which, Breadmores, was to remain in business there for one hundred years. (Its office is now the Kew Bookshop.) The other shops mostly served local needs, gradually establishing a new village centre at what was a natural meeting point between the St Anne's and St Luke's parishes.

This was a logical development, surprising only in that it took so long to emerge. Far more unexpected was that a multi-million business was at the same time being pioneered next door in Station Avenue. This was the development of Rayon. Even now, few people in Kew can identify this little cul-de-sac, and even fewer can probably find the even smaller cul-de-sac of South Avenue, off Sandycombe Road, where the vital discovery was first made.

In 1885 two organic chemists, Charles Cross and Edward Bevan, who had worked at Kew's Jodrell Laboratory and who lived in Kew, became consultants to the paper industry. In 1892 they discovered cellulose xanthate which they named Viscose.

At that time there was a business in South Avenue called the Zurich Incandescent Light Works. Its manager, Charles Stearn, met Cross, who suggested that filaments could be made from his Viscose. The initial experiments were disappointing, but Cross and Stearn found that Viscose made good artificial silk, and set up the Viscose Spinning Syndicate in Station Avenue.

It was to be one of the major discoveries in the textile industry, but Kew was not to benefit from its development. Courtaulds bought the business in 1904. Consequently Viscose became Rayon, and the whole business was sent to Coventry.

125 The first girl gardeners of Kew.

126 The workshop at Station Avenue. Members of the Viscose Spinning Syndicate inside the Kew Works, shortly after Stearn had succeeded in producing the first viscose yarn—known then as Stearn Silk.

Commerce and Kew Green

As Kew grew in size, it changed as well. It became commercial—especially around the Green. From the 1860s, the houses there, built in Georgian times for Georgian gentlemen, were one by one turned into tea rooms, and their pretty riverside gardens filled with tables for the visitors from town.

Those gentlemen and ladies may well have spun in their graves at this development, but effectively there was no great change of use. They too had been in trade. They had served the royal family. There was Mrs. Papendiek, the daughter of a page and herself Assistant Keeper of the Wardrobe and Reader to Her Majesty; there were the Meyers who owed their position and their money to royal patronage. There was Lady Finch, the royal Governess, and Dr. Majendie, a Swiss employed to teach Her Majesty English—which he did surprisingly well.

The one oddity then was the extraordinary Mrs. Schnell who rented no. 77, the Engleheart house. She was, as she apparently told everyone at tedious length, a very superior lady, because she was the goddaughter of the Old Pretender. This was an unusual claim to fame, but especially so on Kew Green which was otherwise occupied entirely by those who depended on the patronage of a royal family that had only kept its power by defeating the two Pretenders in bloody battle. However, Mrs. Schnell, though clearly an appalling bore, was a respected member of the community. She died full of years but in horrific circumstances. Her hair, dressed elaborately in a style that perhaps only her godfather might have recognised, caught fire. Her tomb at St Anne's is equally elaborate.

127 The second Kew Bridge, seen from the Kew bank, with the Brentford Tile and Slate factory in the background.

128 The Dieudonne—one of several tea rooms on Kew Green owned by Will Evans (seen on the left of the postcard).

129 Crowds on the north side of the Green on their way back to London, no doubt via the electric tram or Kew Bridge station.

130 The chair of the Three Kew Bridges. The whereabouts of this chair, created as a gift for Edward VII for the opening of Kew's third bridge in 1903, are now unknown.

131 The Boys Sundial. Mounted on one of the only known surviving balusters of the second Kew Bridge, this oddly shaped sundial was designed to be accurate up to half a minute. At the moment—but surely only temporarily—the Gardens have this remarkable sundial in store.

Her house remained unusual, as unlike its neighbours it was never used as a tea room. The boom in tea rooms peaked in 1903, when the old bridge was rebuilt that year. The old bridge, despite its desperately steep approach, had served its purpose well. It had also, in common with the other bridges on the lower Thames, been freed from tolls in 1873. The new bridge was dramatically different. It was wider—and so required the destruction of buildings on its east and west—and it was far more gentle in its angle of approach. It had a new name too. It was named after the new king, who performed the opening ceremony. It is therefore, officially, called the King Edward VII Bridge, though the name is never used.

At the opening the King was given two presents: a chair commemorating the three Kew Bridges, and—very rare—a bronze axe excavated during the sinking of the new piers (see page 2). Photographs remain, but not the gifts themselves. Perhaps when they are recovered and put on public show, the King may be remembered in Kew with more affection—and bus drivers will be mystified by requests for tickets to the Edward VII Bridge.

The Last of the Market Gardeners

At the turn of the century, the Leyborne-Popham estate was almost unique in that it had remained virtually unchanged from its great days in the 18th and 19th centuries. Most of those who owned land beside the Thames had by then sold out to the developers, partly because of the difficulties faced by their tenants, and partly because of the huge profits to be made from housing. The Leyborne-Popham acres only began to give way in the early 1900s.

There had, of course, been changes. By 1865 half the land had been turned over to growing fruit—even now several residents still have fruit trees planted by the market gardeners—and this seems to have prolonged the viability of the business for a few more years. Certainly at the end of the century the two major market gardeners, John Poupart and James Pocock, were doing well enough to be living themselves at West Park and West Hall. Even Poupart and Pocock though had no chance of matching the offers of the developers, and

132 Leyborne Park, where Edwardian houses commemorate the family that once owned the estate.

gradually now they gave up fields as one by one new streets began to appear.

One of the first to be developed, in 1902, was appropriately entitled Leyborne Park, after the owners of the land. This was on the edge of the estate, and backed on to the Englehearts' Cumberland Road. At one end of this new road there was already a house, the old farmhouse used by the market gardener, Richard Atwood. Now it was occupied by Richard's son, Frederick, a well-established surveyor, who by a strange twist of fate was now employed by the Leyborne-Pophams to supervise the development of the estate. He called his own house Leyborne Lodge.

Leyborne Park marked the old boundary between the parish of Kew and the manor of East Sheen and West Hall. The southern end of the boundary had already been developed, mostly in the 1880s, with a long line of houses along the eastern side of Sandycombe Road. Most of these were built in terraces. (One, Grayson Terrace, commemorated for years the extraordinary grower of asparagus; now sadly the name has fallen as he did.) From 1901 the other side of the new railway line also began to be developed, the track beside the railway becoming North Road. At its southern end appeared a cluster of small roads with small houses and even smaller shops, most of the shops being in North Road itself, but with a few in Lytchett Terrace which was built alongside the road that led to Richmond from Mortlake.

It is probable that Frederick Atwood chose the names of these streets and the others that over the next 20 years gradually spread over the estate. Several of them would be named after the current owners (Leyborne and Popham), or the estates they held (Pensford, Chilton, Chelwood, Marksbury, and probably Niton), one after the previous owners (Taylor). Only Dancer Road is named after a market gardener, either Mr. Dancer who grew asparagus here, or his widow. It is remarkable how many master market gardeners died young, with their fields being subsequently farmed by their widows or daughters. Market gardening was an exacting business—too much so for several of the men.

133 *(facing page)* Hugh Leyborne-Popham, who gave the site of the Barn Church to those who now live on his family's estate. (See page 122.)

110

The Birth of the Union

Kew seems to have greeted its incorporation into the new Borough of Richmond with something like relief. As in all small parishes, Kew's Vestrymen had been finding it increasingly difficult to handle all the responsibilities thrust upon them. There were not only the roads, the poor, the sewers and the endless new regulations for them to worry over; at one time there had even been requirements that some of them act as tax collectors for central government. Consequently there had been a series of cases where various market gardeners, bakers, and publicans had failed to hand over to government money that they had been required to collect—generally because their own businesses had been at that time on the verge of bankruptcy. Sometimes the Vestry had stepped in to bail them out. At other times it had decided that the local citizen was not worth the cost.

The new boroughs took on most of these responsibilities, and left the parishes uncertain as to what rôle they should now play. In the new housing developments on the old Selwyn and Leyborne-Popham estates this was no great issue, as the new householders had scarcely begun to establish a community spirit, but Kew parish clearly felt at a loss. In 1901 the leading citizens in the new Kew Ward decided that they needed now to act as a pressure group on the Council; otherwise their interests might go by default. With this in mind, they reconstituted their old ratepayers society as the Kew Union.

This Union, open to all ratepayers in Kew (480 in 1901), held public meetings to discuss matters of concern to the members. They voted on what they wanted the Borough to do, and they selected candidates for the elections. (Kew had three Councillors, and generally an Alderman as well.) Until 1939 their candidates were elected unopposed.

Their chief concern was the tramway from Kew Bridge along the Kew Road. It was vital to the commercial and social health of the village, but it was mostly either ill-maintained or—far worse—under threat of being transformed into an electric tramway. The pond, then as now, was both an environmental asset and a health hazard. The fire engine, even more essential to the safety of the village, was an even more urgent subject of debate.

134 *(above)* Kew Green in 1905, just after the completion of the new bridge.

135 *(right)* The horse trams. The tram service ran from 1883 to 1912 from Kew Bridge to the *Orange Tree* in Richmond. Here the tram is passing the new Victoria Gate.

The engine was housed in one corner of the village, its horse in another, and the fireman in yet another. Luckily there was never a major fire to test out the effectiveness of this peculiar arrangement, but the Union argued long and hard over how to amend it.

Naturally the Union, working through its Councillors, did not always persuade the Council to do what it wanted—it would take them, for instance, 60 years to get the branch library they first campaigned for in 1906! Still, it was a radical experiment in community politics well in advance of its time.

The New Schools

On 19 October 1905, all the dignitaries of the new Richmond Council gathered with due ceremony to watch the Mayor lay the foundation stone of the Borough's first elementary schools. The site chosen was in the new development at the south end of the Leyborne-Popham estate. They were to be named the Darrell Road Schools. Oddly, however, when the even more important opening ceremony took place in 1906, the spelling had subtly changed. The schools were named the Darell Road Schools.

It has taken many years for everyone to catch up with the change of name, but now both road and schools are Darell. It is still uncertain why the change was made.

There is no doubt that the road was first called Darrell, though it was the most unexpected of the names chosen by Atwood for the new roads on the Leyborne-Popham estate. William Darrell in the 16th century was the owner of the magnificent house of Littlecote in Wiltshire. He was also at best a wastrel and at worst a murderer. Darrell somehow avoided retribution for the latter—

accusations of murder in those days could be, and very often were, brushed aside by great landowners—but the consequences of his spendthrift style of life were far more dire. To cope with his lack of funds, he effectively mortgaged his house simultaneously to two wealthy neighbours, so that when he died comparatively young they had to sort out which had the right of succession to his property. Success and succession went to the Pophams, who from then on based themselves at Littlecote.

We must assume that the family approved of Atwood's choice of this name for one of the new roads, but he and they may well have been commemorating, not William, but Wild Darrell, the family's Derby winner. If so, the joke backfired. Perhaps Richmond Council thought they would be mocked if their first schools were known to be named after either a horse or a rake. Anyway they had an easy solution. Richmond had a great landowning family of its own called Darell. Sir Lionel Darell had been a close friend of George III, and had lived at Ancaster House by the Richmond

136 Gainsborough School.

114

137   The opening of the Darell Road Schools.

entrance to the Park. His family owned property throughout Richmond, and even in Kew. (John Dillman had indeed purchased some of his Kew Road land from John Darell.)

This little confusion might have appeared an uneasy omen for a new school, but in fact the school flourished, and never more so than recently: it has received national recognition for its teaching—particularly of reading. Perhaps the ability to distinguish between Darrell and Darell is useful training.

Some twenty years after the opening of Darell, a second state school was sited in Kew. This was far larger. It was a secondary school, and it was set at the southern end of the Selwyn estate. This was the last part of the estate to be developed. It had been bought by the local authority for council housing, and was initially laid out between 1912 and 1913 with names chosen by the Borough Librarian. It is therefore thanks to him that this end of Kew primarily commemorates local celebrities: Robert Dudley; the author, Mary Braddon; the diplomat, Sir William Temple. The longest road was named after Gainsborough. So later was the school.

Gainsborough School served the whole borough well for some fifty years, first as a Central School, and then as a Secondary Modern. However, when the Borough adopted comprehensive education in 1970s it was found to have one irredeemable disadvantage: it was too small. It was pulled down and the site was sold for housing. Only its weathervane remains, perched defiantly on a hut in the middle of the estate.

Kew in the First World War

Like other British villages, Kew has its own long lists of those who died in the First World War. They are commemorated at St Anne's and St Luke's. Among them was a VC, Captain William Johnston RE, who won the medal only a year before he was killed. A garden was created down on the Westerly Ware and dedicated to the memory of all who died.

It was not, however, just men that Kew sent to war. They sent aeroplanes as well. Further downriver, on the meadow-land that Sir William Hooker had once let out for £50 a year, the Glendower Aircraft Company established what was the first sizable industrial operation in Kew, a factory which built initially De Haviland DH4 light biplane bombers, and then Salamanders. Virginia Woolf recorded in her diaries that a Zeppelin dropped a bomb on Kew. In fact, it fell north of the bridge, but the Germans might have been aiming at the factory.

All villages, of course, have similar memories and memorials. Yet Kew had something extra to commemorate. During the war it became a mecca for ministers, bishops, prime ministers, and innumerable members of the royal family. They came not to visit the Gardens, nor any of the elegant houses round the Green, but what is now and was even then the least prepossessing building in the whole of Kew—the Victoria Working Men's Club, on the east side of Sandycombe Road.

This building, like the club, has an unusual history. Built mostly of corrugated iron, it was from 1876 to 1889 the 'iron church' that housed both St Luke's church and St Luke's school. When the new church was built in the Avenue, the iron building was moved across the road to make room for the new school buildings. In 1892 it was opened as a social club.

As its president, it had the influential Alderman Szlumper, a retired engineer, and one-time Mayor of Richmond. However, the story is that it was not the Alderman that first attracted royalty to visit the club, but a member who had been employed as a builder at Buckingham Palace. He

138 The Victoria Working Men's Club, with the original church window still in place.

139 The last of the royal visitors to the club—George VI and Queen Elizabeth.

140 The old Tea House in Kew Gardens. The sender of this postcard wrote: 'This is the original tea house as it was before being burnt down by the *wild women*'. It had been burnt down by two suffragettes in 1913! The new tea house was built in 1915.

apparently persuaded the Prince of Wales to attend the annual dinner, and the Prince in turn persuaded his parents to visit it too. It seems from the club's annual reports that the club then became famous for the amount of money it raised to send cigarettes to men at the front, and it was presumably this that attracted visits from no less than four overseas prime ministers, and innumerable British ministers and members of the royal family. In all, the club boasted of visits from 50 such VIPs over seven years—probably a unique record for a club of its size, and most certainly for one set in such accommodation.

The club retained its royal connections up to the next war, but eventually closed in the 1980s. Despite its stirring history, the building has not been listed!

Death and Destruction by Water and by Wind

It is perhaps unfair to describe the old iron church as Kew's most unprepossessing building. There is another that is far less attractive, but it is not on the same scale. This is Kew's own mortuary. It is set ironically just opposite the War Memorial Garden, and it is hard to understand why it was left standing when the Garden was laid out. According to the Union's minutes, its 'use had been discontinued' in 1914.

This 'use' had been as a temporary resting place for bodies washed up on the side of the river, a fairly common occurrence at one time. There are still accidents and suicides, but recovery of the bodies is now handled with more despatch; so the mortuary stands empty—of corpses, anyway. Had it not been closed, though, it might have welcomed a very distinguished body in March 1920, that of Edith Holden, author of *The Country Diary of an Edwardian Lady*.

Edith Holden drowned, not in the river, but in the ha-ha that lies between the towpath and Kew Gardens. It seems that her interest in nature was most probably the cause of her accident, as she was picking chestnut buds at the time, and seems to have slipped.

The press coverage of Edith Holden's inquest was not extensive, as her artistic talents were known only to a few friends at the time of her death. Death by drowning anyway rates a minimum of column inches. Floods, however, are quite another matter, and Kew had extensive coverage when hit by floods in 1928. Though they caused no deaths, they caused considerable damage to property. Five hundred houses were inundated, and the Mayor opened a fund for the relief of the victims.

There had been similar floods in previous centuries, but they had given rise to very little comment, as the land they covered then was mostly water meadow. In the 20th century, however, with housing built close to the towpath, something akin to a war was being waged along the riverside between man and nature.

In all, there were to be four such floods in Kew, and between the floods, even if the water did not come over the towpath, it was quite likely

---

DROWNED IN THE HA-HA

The accidental death of a Chelsea woman, Mrs. Edith Smith, of 2, Oakley-crescent, was the subject of an inquest conducted at Richmond on Thursday by Dr. M. H. Taylor.

Alfred Smith identified the body as that of his wife, aged 47. He last saw her at a quarter-past eight on Monday morning. When he returned he found the table ready laid, and he thought she had gone to see some friends. She had complained in the morning of a headache, and witness advised her to go for a walk, and she said she would go Putney way. His wife had no trouble so far as he knew. She was a painter and in order to get materials for her work she occasionally collected twigs. On Tuesday morning he became uneasy and informed the police.

Police-constable Cattle said as he was walking down by the water side early on Tuesday morning near Kew Gardens wall, some fifty yards from the Old Deer Park Gardens, he saw deceased lying face downwards in four feet of water in the Ha-Ha. In her hand was a bunch of twigs. It appeared as though she had been pulling down the branch of the tree with an umbrella when she fell into the water. He removed the body and then sent for the police surgeon, who pronounced life to be extinct.

Dr. Pain deposed that death was due to drowning. There were no marks of violence and there were no bruises or injuries. He would think that she had been in the water quite sixteen hours.

A verdict in accordance with the medical evidence was returned.

The cremation of the remains took place at Golders Green yesterday afternoon, the service being conducted by the Rev. Basil Martin, North Finchley. Messrs. T. H. Saunders and Sons, Kew-Road, were the undertakers.

141   The local press report on Edith Holden's death.

---

to well up through the gratings in the streets. The towpath was raised repeatedly and this, along with the Thames barrier, has now tipped the odds in favour of the houses. Even so, the river can boast major battle honours—the floods of 1928, 1947, 1953 and 1965 left scars and memories in Kew that will not be easily forgotten.

142 The Temple of the Sun. This beautiful building, built in 1761, was destroyed in 1916 by the fall of the even older cedar beside it, grown from seed by the Duke of Argyll in 1725.

143 Ruskin Avenue in the floods of 1928.

Roads and Cemeteries

Kew, like most small communities, has fought long, hard, and often bitter battles against plans to widen roads, especially if they threatened shops and old buildings. It is disconcerting—and salutary—to note that not so long ago the position was reversed. Local pressure then was often in favour of wider roads, even at the cost of shops and ancient houses.

Although the Kew Union always fought against any suggestion that electric trams might run through the village, it still pressed urgently for the widening of Kew Road, largely because pedestrians were being splashed by passing (mostly horse-drawn) traffic. It also argued for the widening of the junction with Mortlake Road, chiefly because it was considered dangerous. Until it was widened, the Union insisted that a constable be kept on duty there.

The Borough Council were persuaded. First, in 1915, they bought up and demolished a row of 18th-century cottages and shops, to enable them to widen the northern end of Kew Road. (See picture on page 92.) Then in 1929 they removed another row of shops, including that of the Taylor family, as well as most of the garden of Descanso House, to widen the 'dangerous' junction.

In 1927 when the decision was announced, the Kew Union formally congratulated its Councillors and the Council. However, at the very same meeting it showed itself far less enthusiastic about plans for road widening elsewhere.

This other road widening was along the Lower Richmond Road, to establish a broad route from Richmond to the new Chiswick Bridge, which was due to open in 1933. Here again, shops and small houses had to go, including Lytchett Terrace, built less than thirty years before on the edge of the Leyborne-Popham estate. It was suggested that the dispossessed tenants be accommodated in new Council housing to be built on the site of Gloucester House. (For years the big house had been run as a school for Jewish girls by the Neumegen family, but the school and the Neumegens were now long gone, and the site was ripe for development.)

There was a howl of protest from the Union: 'A working class colony in a highly rated locality would be very detrimental to the rateable value of the surrounding property,' it said. The dispossessed were the concern of North Ward, not of Kew Ward. The Union won, and Gloucester

144 The junction of the Kew and Mortlake roads, before the widening of 1929 removed several shops and cottages, including the Taylors' bakery and post office.

145 The Chiswick Bridge and the cemeteries before the bridge was opened in 1933.

House gave way to Gloucester Court's emphatically private flats.

Lytchett Terrace was not the only victim of the widening of the Lower Mortlake and Lower Richmond Roads. Its route was past Pink's Farm, where William Atwood had lived. For a short time the farm remained, overshadowed by the new embankment to the bridge; then it was pulled down. It no longer had any land around it. The road and—to a far greater extent—the cemeteries had taken all the fields.

These cemeteries were a phenomenon of the early 1900s. By then churchyards were full to overflowing. Some, like that of St Anne's, had been so for almost two centuries. That was why Kirby's extension in 1770—less than sixty years after the chapel was built—had allowed for a bone store.

New graves could only be provided in spaces occupied by older bones, which were first stored and then disposed of by way of bon(e)fires. It was highly unsatisfactory, and the government eventually stepped in and insisted that such graveyards be closed and new cemeteries be provided. With the recent rush to build houses, some boroughs had to look beyond their own boundaries for sites, and then pay competitive prices. So the Leyborne-Pophams had found themselves selling land for cemeteries, not just to Richmond but also to Fulham.

Now more of their land went to build the road. The planners no doubt thought the price they paid worth while. Elsewhere along the route they had faced opposition over the noise the road would bring. Here at least there would be no problems. The dead would not complain.

The Coming of the Barn

Paradoxically it could be argued that the oldest building in Kew is neither Kew Palace nor West Hall, but a building that arrived in the village as late as 1929. This is the Barn Church of St Philip and All Saints, built from a barn the beams of which were brought to its new site—like a prefab—on the back of lorries.

In 1929 St Philip and All Saints was unique, the only church in Britain to be built, as it were, from a recycled barn. Although there had been earlier barn churches in Normandy—and at least three others have since been built in this country—in 1929 the very concept of a barn church was unfamiliar in Britain. So the credit for its conception as well as its construction is due to the owners of the original barn, the Lamberts of Oxted, a village at the opposite corner of Surrey.

Uvedale Lambert was a devout Christian, very much aware that there was a desperate need for new churches in the 1920s to cater for the new housing estates. He also had a barn that he no longer used. Over three centuries it had provided both for food and drink. Primarily, it had stored grain; then, when corn was no longer profitable, Lambert had used it himself briefly for the hops he grew. Now it was derelict. Impressed by a friend's description of barns as 'the cathedrals of agriculture', he offered the barn to his diocese.

Dr. Garbett, Bishop of Southwark, imaginatively seized on the offer. He had in North Sheen an area with houses, but no church. On the other hand, he did have a congregation. Since 1910 a small group had been meeting at a mission hall, St Peter's, in Chilton Road under the aegis of the new St Luke's parish. It even had its own priest-in-charge. There was also a site. Although the Leyborne-Pophams had not allowed for shops or a pub in the centre of their development, they had left space for a church. Garbett then found that Mrs. Lambert's relations, the Hoares, who had once owned land in Mortlake, would also like to help. As the Hoares owned a merchant bank, that help could be considerable.

It was a medieval situation—typical of those once illustrated in stained-glass windows. Here were three families eager to build a church: the Leyborne-Pophams with the land, the Lamberts the essential beams, and the Hoares the rest of the

146 The Lamberts' L-shaped barn at Oxted being dismantled ...

147 ... and being reassembled as the Barn Church. (Each beam was carefully numbered; the numbers are still clearly visible.)

building materials. (One of the Hoare relations owned a brickworks in Basingstoke, which created bricks of a 17th-century pattern to match the beams.) The parish itself raised money for most of the furniture.

In record time, and at record low cost to the diocese, the Barn was ready for dedication on 4 February 1929, since when it has served a parish—part owner-occupied, part Council estate—that has increased steadily in size year by year. It is, of course, one of the youngest parishes in the area, but the beams under which its parishioners worship are almost certainly ships' timbers of the 16th century, and very possibly from ships that fought the Armada. As such, they are at least the equals of that aristocratic elm under which Elizabeth met Leicester.

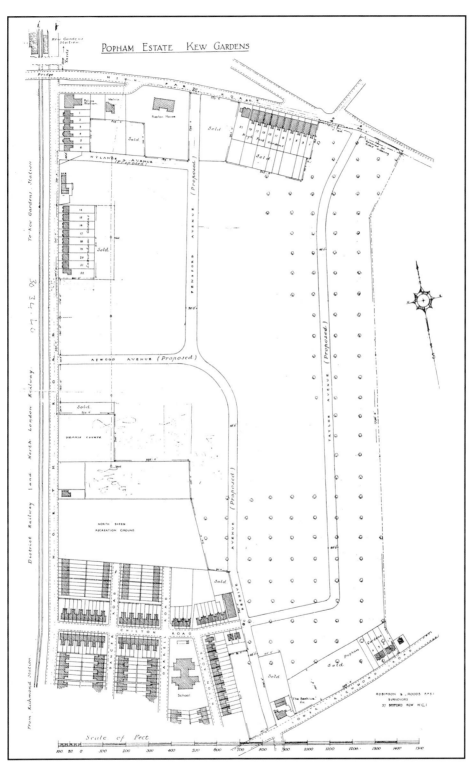

148 North Sheen in the 1920s. The large house of 'Reston', built in memory of a son lost in the First World War, occupied most of the land between Nylands Avenue and High Park Road.

The Legacy of the Leyborne-Pophams

The arrival of the Barn Church was an essential catalyst in the development of the Leyborne-Popham estate. Up to 1930, building there had been tentative—even hesitant. Certainly much of the market gardens' land had gone for housing, but it had gone piecemeal. There had been the first houses around Darell Road. There had then been the gradual centipetal development around the station—Leyborne, Beechwood, Burlington, Defoe and Ruskin.

Meanwhile houses had spread along the Mortlake Road, closing steadily in on the old house of West Park. The tide proved irresistible. Hooker's garden became West Park Avenue and the house itself was pulled down—or most of it. One wing remains, and so does the old drive. The drive, however, no longer winds between lawns but directly to a small industrial estate, where unmistakable, though cruelly changed, the remnants of the 17th-century house now accommodate offices and workrooms.

Apart from the loss of West Park, the surrounding hamlet remained almost unaltered.

West Hall was there and so were its 18th-century neighbours, West Lodge and West Farm. As for the market gardeners, the Pouparts and the Pococks had gone, but the Bessant sisters were still at Brick Farm.

149   The Iron Bridge on the towpath in 1895, drawn by Albert Betts. The bridge spanned the entrance to the drainage works docks, where once the dung barges used to discharge their loads.

150   West Park in 1903.

151 William Thompson, when mayor of Richmond in 1908.

The riverside, however, had altered significantly. Much of it was covered as before with lettuces and radishes, but there were substantial buildings too. There had clearly been plans for more literary roads beyond Ruskin, but they had been abandoned, and the Ministry of Labour had built temporary offices there for the handling of National Insurance. Down river, Dodge were making cars where Glendower had built aeroplanes, and the Sewage Works were sited where once the dung barges had dumped their loads. There was also the tall chimney of the Dust—a rubbish destructor put up by Barnes, the local authority for this corner of the estate. And of course there were the cemeteries.

What was left of the centre of the estate had been mostly turned over to fruit trees and bushes, but with the arrival of the Barn Church this was rapidly covered with new housing, as the last of the Leyborne-Pophams sold off the last of the old estate. Houses spread rapidly along Taylor, Marksbury, Pensford and Atwood Avenues—the last commemorating the family that had farmed and then surveyed the estate.

There were also other new roads with significantly different names—those developed by the Council. Chaucer and Garrick recalled Richmond's artistic heritage, while Thompson commemorated a more recent hero. William Thompson was a radical local politician, for many years Councillor for North Ward. He had, however, a national reputation, as in 1896 he had been responsible for some of the first council housing in the country—the Manor Grove estate on the other side of the main road from Kew.

The Last of the Old Trades

By the 1930s the peninsula of Kew was in danger of gaining the whole world, while losing its own soul. Its Gardens were feted internationally as unique. Its roads were lined with the best in contemporary domestic architecture. Yet, apart from the Gardens, it had hardly any local industry: almost all its residents worked elsewhere. The whole peninsula was on the way to becoming no more than a dormitory development.

To some this did not matter too much. Most of those who had moved into the new housing were not looking for a village atmosphere—they were running away from it. They were happy just to be part of the Richmond Borough—so long as the trains ran to time.

Many, however, especially those around the Green, were deeply unhappy at the change of atmosphere. They were of Kew, and wanted to work within Kew. Sadly though, most of the traditional trades had gone. There were no more fish to fish, and no one wanted baskets made from osiers. A few seized the chance of working for the Ministry of Labour, or with Dodge. There was also Hickey's Steam Engine works in Sandycombe Road. Others worked, but mostly part time, for what were left of the market gardens.

There was still work to be had in domestic service—some of it residential in the larger houses—and a few opportunities in the retail trades. The restaurants round the Green—some of them even offering hotel facilities—flourished until 1940, before reverting to their original purpose as family houses. After that only one of the great tea houses survived, and it was not on the Green, but in Kew Road—the Newens' Maids of Honour Shop which sold—and still retains the secret recipe for—the famous tartlets created for Queen Caroline.

By then Kew had lost its last blacksmith. This was J. Attfield whose forge was swept away by the building of the third Kew bridge. He found another farrier's shop at the other side of the bridge. His son, Jim Attfield, in later years a local Councillor, and a manager of the Queen's School until the 1970s, was seven at the time.

'Horses used to be stabled behind the Coach and Horses,' he recalled. 'Provision people called Fullers kept four horses there, Tyne Main Coal kept eight, and the landlord kept two.

152 Attfield's forge just before it was swept away to accommodate the new wide bridge of 1903. The building beyond is now part of Caxton Name Plate Manufacturing.

153 Delivering Newens' bread by handcart.

154 Hickey's Steam Engine Works, with North Road in the background.

'My brother and I, even before we went to school, had to come over and fetch the horses, and before we took them over to the forge we used to have a gallop round the Green and see who would win. Aldous, the landlord of the *Coach and Horses*, had a very sprightly horse that very nearly put me over the parapet of the bridge.

'The Green then had high posts all round, like those round the little green by the Gardens gate. At that time there were cows and horses grazing there, and over by the Church there was a kind of barred gate which could be opened to let them in and out. Mr Beech used to keep the fairground then, and many a time when I began to work for my father I would go there to trim the horses' hooves.'

At the time there were over thirty blacksmiths in Richmond and Brentford. When Jim himself retired in the 1960s—just before Mr. Beech's roundabouts finally ground to a halt—there was only one.

155 Beech's fairground in 1952, with the grounds of the *Boat House* hotel on the left.

The Second World War

For Kew the First World War had been mostly a matter for mourning and money-raising for the boys 'over there'. The Second, however, was cause for more immediate shock and horror. The records of bombs kept by the ARP service give some idea of what Kew residents endured.

> Bombs: High Explosive 59; Incendiaries 44; Phosphorous 5; Oil 3; Mines 3; V1 1; V2 1. Houses destroyed: 44.

Compared with what the East End or Coventry suffered, this was nothing, but it was still far above the average loss of other villages. Yet those who lived through those times recall them with a certain macabre relish.

The worst of the bombs was the last: a V2 that destroyed eight houses in West Park Avenue on the morning of 12 September 1944. It also caused considerable damage to the Chrysler factory, which had succeeded Dodge and had been assembling fuselages, first for Halifaxes and then for Lancasters—very much as the Glendower factory had done in the First World War.

One of the houses hit belonged to the Fortune family, who luckily were away that night. They had been there throughout 1939 and 1940: 'In the Blitz we could read by the glare,' Mrs. Fortune recalls. 'There was a siren at the same time every night and we used to go to the cellar under Robbins. My husband was then moved to Harrogate, and I got a job there too. Every time we came back to Kew, a bomb came down. One fell by the Barn, in a bit of market garden—at end of Taylor. Then another little bomb fell a few doors away.

156 Beechwood Avenue at war. With the exception of West Park Avenue, Beechwood was the unluckiest road in Kew. In 1940 it was hit in five raids and lost a total of eight houses.

157 The Herbarium at war.

'The V2 destroyed eight houses, and left its crater in the soft gardens at the back of the houses. It was the second to fall on London—the first fell on Gunnersbury—but it was announced as a gas explosion. The authorities may have known, but we didn't.'

Many of those in the larger houses had left them for the duration; so there were fewer people around. On the other hand there was also a small number of refugees, and an even larger number of servicemen housed in the old Ministry of Labour offices. First there were RAF, then GIs, and finally Italian POWs, some of whom—and especially the last—struck up lifelong friendships with Kew people.

The Green by then was honeycombed with air-raid shelters, which offered not only safety during the Blitz but infinite entertainment to the children subsequently. Also much of it—but not the cricket square—was used for allotments as part of the campaign to 'Dig for Victory'.

At the same time the Green lost its iron railings for scrap, except for the railings around the little triangle by the Main Gates, which remain now as they were. This peculiar exemption from the war-effort was apparently because this was royal land—

158 A wartime service at Chrysler's Aircraft Factory.

an odd decision in view of Queen Mary's well known enthusiasm for collecting scrap. (At Badminton in Gloucestershire she was renowned for seizing any plough or harrow left untended in the fields, and they had later to be returned surreptitiously to the indignant farmers.) She would never have hesitated to take the rails from outside her grandparents' old home.

Rising Fortunes

159 An unblemished stretch of Victorian houses in Kew Road ...

160 ... and *(inset)* a typical replacement.

After the Second World War radical change was fashionable. There was a new trend—even amongst the comfortably off—for simple self-sufficient housing. People wanted well-equipped flats, not rambling Victorian family homes.

In Kew, from the 1950s to the 1960s, the developers moved in on the big Victorian detached houses in and around the Kew Road. For the owners, many of whom had no great emotional ties with the old houses—they had been away during most of the war—the offers were irresistible.

The impact on Kew was devastating. Kew Road's houses were hardly old compared with the Georgian ones on the Green, but they had become part of the landscape. The shock, however, could have been far worse. Elsewhere in Britain the new aspirations led to high-rise flats, but this was not allowed in the Borough of Richmond, and certainly not in Kew. Every plan for high-rise development was rejected.

As late as the 1970s there was an application to build a large hotel on the site of the riverside *Boat House*, a down-at-heel pub with a rather raffish reputation. As a local councillor said, the danger was not so much the 13-storey plan they first submitted, but the nine-storey plan they would offer as a compromise. In the event neither was accepted. Only across the river in Brentford was tall considered beautiful.

Kew's blocks of flats are all of a modest height and bulk. Now they are very much part of the scenery, though many of the flat dwellers move on too swiftly to become part of the community—except in one corner of Kew. This is where Grayson and the Bessants had once lived.

Brick Stables is now Brick Farm Close; and Hawthorn and Magnolia Courts stand where hawthorn bushes and magnolia trees once clustered around West Hall. These flats were built by the Council in the 1960s, and they have a distinct character of their own. They and their residents are very much part of the community, and they inherit something of the sturdy independence of their market gardener forebears.

Political Upheaval

Kew's new flats not only introduced a change in the look of Kew Road, they also signalled a change in the character of the village. Where previously the old Kew parish had been at least equal in population to the parishes of St Luke's and the Barn, and certainly senior in experience, now it was definitely smaller and less influential. A further shock was also in train. With the creation of the Greater London Council in 1965, Kew was politically transformed. For many years it had had three small wards: Kew, St Luke's and North Sheen. Now they were amalgamated into the single large ward of Kew.

This in effect formalised what had been long accepted. The whole peninsula was now all Kew. Nearly everyone in the new ward was happy with their name, but many were far from happy with the electoral implications. At the time, St Luke's ward had Labour councillors, and North Sheen Liberals, while for the last sixty years Kew Green had returned 'Independent' councillors pre-selected by the Kew Union (now known as Kew Ratepayers).

What would happen with this new Council and this new large ward, especially in view of the influx of flat dwellers? (The electorate was now almost 7,000.) The answer was that the Independents, the Labour and the Liberal candidates all lost out. In 1968 Kew went Conservative. So did the whole of the new Council of Richmond upon Thames.

For some, it was the end of an era, for others the beginning. Kew Ratepayers almost immediately dropped out of what had become a party political battle. Under the presidency of George Cassidy, one of their longest serving councillors and a distinguished historian of Kew, the Ratepayers became the Kew (Amenity) Society. Meanwhile the Liberals, whose leader Jo Grimond lived on Kew Green, reacted to their own electoral defeat by adopting and refining the philosophy of parish pump politics, and set out to recreate over the whole of Kew the sense of community that had been the essential element of first the old Kew Vestry and then the Kew Union.

The Liberals' national commitment to Community Politics, as this was called, was at first patchy, largely because it grew out of individual, independent, initiatives all over the country. Arguably the most influential of these was in Kew. Its most effective champion was Dr. Stanley Rundle, who first broke the Tory monopoly by winning a by-election, and then set in train a political bandwagon that would eventually lead to the Liberal Democrats in 1986 taking 49 of the 52 seats on the Council, almost reversing the situation of 1968. Rundle himself died in 1979, but not before winning a seat himself on the Greater London Council, at which time the three leaders of the Liberal Parliamentary, GLC and Richmond upon Thames groups all lived within half a mile of each other in Kew.

Kew politics in the 1970s and 1980s turned largely on the defensive campaigns it fought against the two greatest threats to its environment—cars and airplanes—but at the same time there were gains to be snatched from the teeth of adversity. When the small St Luke's school had to close and the big St Luke's church became a burden to maintain, the community of Kew reacted as one.

161 Stanley Rundle.

131

162 St Luke's House Educational Centre, developed from the former Church of England Primary School.

Committees were formed, money raised, the Council spurred to action. The buildings were spared, the school being adapted as an Education Centre, and the church altered to accommodate a day centre. The ghosts of innumerable Vestrymen and Independent councillors must surely have joined in the celebrations.

Sports and Leisure

Some villages are known, or would like to be known, for their sporting achievements. They have made their names perhaps in football leagues, in bowls or snooker. Kew, of course, has its football, its bowls clubs, and its snooker too (at the Kew Men's Social Club, which has been based at the *Coach and Horses* for some 70 years). Kew has had its own heroes too—some in unexpected sports, as with the gold medal won as a pentathlete by Kew Gardens student Danny Nightingale in the 1976 Olympics—but generally Kew seems to have shared the Olympic vision. It is less interested in winning than in taking part, and most of its favourite activities are rooted deeply in its past.

One of them, cricket, is almost as deeply rooted as it was in Hambledon—as we know from the best possible source, those who thought it worth their criticism. Soon after Prince Frederick established Kew Green as the fashionable place for cricket—and therefore for gambling—a London newspaper wrote that a striking example of 'the cursed spirit of Gaming, Idleness and Extravagance' could now be seen at Kew Green where two or three hundred men, most of them labourers, assemble 'to divert themselves with playing at the game of cricket'. Although these labourers had been earnestly solicited to assist in the harvest field, and were tempted with an offer of five shillings for each day, they had absolutely refused to work.

So it was not only the great that were guilty! But one wonders exactly where they pitched their wickets in those days, as the road to the ferry cut straight across the Green. Perhaps they were less fussy then about the surface. Happily there is an unbroken tradition of cricket on the Green since the mid-1700s, culminating in the current charity matches starring showbiz stars, some of them even more famous than Prince Frederick.

At the other end of Kew there has been for many years a centre for a very different sport. Rowing clubs have established themselves on the riverbank close to the old Pink's Farm. For many

163 Kew Cricket Club 1874.

133

The Old Inns of Kew

years these famous amateur clubs were balanced by a still more amateur group of watermen further upstream—those in the tradition of *Three Men in a Boat*, who hired rowing boats and skiffs from the towpath by Kew Bridge. The hire boats have now been replaced by private motorboats and houseboats, but arguably the river is just as busy now as it was when the medieval barges used it as a highway.

One leisure pursuit, though, is even older than rowing. On Short Lots, once cultivated in strips by Kew peasants, and later (see page 69) handed over to George IV by the Enclosure Act, allotments now recreate something of the pattern of medieval cultivation. Then cultivation was a matter of life or death, but some of those who exhibit at Kew's annual horticultural show would, in the words of a certain football manager, claim that it is now far more important than that!

164 *(top left)* Allotments prizewinners in 1949, with from left to right: G. Cassidy, C. Ricketts, R. Charles, J. Attfield.

165 *(bottom left)* Boats for hire at the end of Bush Road.

Kew has always been well equipped with pubs, and many of them have ancient histories. However, they have tended to cluster together and so have left great acres of the village almost a mile from the nearest watering hole. Part of the blame lies with the Leyborne-Pophams. They carefully reserved a place for a church on their estate, but left all the shops and the only pub out on the perimeter. Now the one pub they did allow has gone.

It lay at the end of Marksbury Avenue, and had been there since at least 1851. Initially it was little more than an alehouse for the itinerant labourers, and was run by three generations of the Saunders family. Rebuilt as the *Beehive*, it flourished till the 1980s when it made way for housing.

There were many others that fell along the way. On the Kew Road, in the 19th century, there were for a time both the *Royal Standard*, at the end of James's Cottages, and the *Cumberland Arms* at no. 274 Kew Road. On the ait, until bought up and closed down by Mr. Hunter, there was the *Swan*, renowned for its eels and its noisy clientele. On the Green, in the 18th century, where now there is a sub post-office, there were first the *Cock*

166 The *Beehive* in 1909.

135

167 The *Coach and Horses* in 1900.

and *Hoop* and then the *Ewe and Lamb*. There were also, somewhere on the Green, the *Rose* and the *Peter Boat*.

All Kew's surviving pubs, apart from the *Kew Gardens Hotel* (in Sandycombe Road) and the *Flower and Firkin* (in the old station buffet), lie now around the Green.

The youngest is the *Greyhound*. Its site was first used as an inn in the 1850s. It was rebuilt in 1937.

Next in order of seniority is the *King's Arms* (now the Kleftiko Restaurant). It was opened in 1772, soon after the first bridge was built. It has never had to move, though it was rebuilt when the house next door came down for the rebuilding of the bridge in 1903.

The *Coach and Horses* is a little older. It was originally at no. 11, opposite the church, where it seems to have succeeded an earlier pub called the *Rising Sun*. It moved across the road about 1771.

The oldest is the *Rose and Crown*, and it has a puzzling history. In 1738 it was definitely on its present site. Then it was based in some old cottages, which were adapted over the years, until a new building was put up in the 1930s. The puzzle lies in where it was originally.

There is a picture showing it 100 yards downstream where Attfield had his forge. Yet there is no

168 The *Rose and Crown*. This drawing is responsible for the belief that in the 18th century the *Rose and Crown* was on the site later occupied by Attfield's forge (see page 136).

record of any pub on that site. Could it be that the artist was misled by the elaborate display of Attfield's 'By appointment' sign (see page 126), and thought it indicated a *Rose and Crown*? It is in fact more likely that it started in Hell House, where its licensee lived from 1726 to 1728, before subletting Hell House to the schoolmaster James Smith. 'Hell House' might well have been an appropriate description. It would be sad if the house got its name from its reputation as a school.

Royalty Returns Again

The story of Kew has been the story of the three Rs: River, Royalty and Railway. Kew would never have begun without the first, flourished without the second, nor grown as it did without the third. In the 1990s, unexpectedly, it is still along the Riverside, despite the collapse of fishing and the closure of the ferry, that there are the most dramatic developments.

Downriver on the old water meadows there is a new Inland Revenue centre—no longer in the pre-fabs that welcomed the soldiers and POWs of the Second World War, but in a handsome post-modernist building of its own. There is also, infinitely larger, the massive Public Record Office—for Kew, indelibly associated with the nation's botanical records, is now also home to the nation's public records. The PRO has been built at the end of Ruskin Avenue, on the fields where children in the Second World War scrumped radishes, and its main building, 'Fort Ruskin', resembles in style the war-time block-house which still clings to the side of the railway embankment.

Upriver, there are new buildings too in the Gardens themselves: the Princess of Wales Conservatory and the Sir Joseph Banks Building, as well as beautifully restored editions of the Palm and the Temperate Houses. This renovation is some comfort—though not a lot—to local residents who now find that they have to pay £4 to enter the Gardens. They look back nostalgically to the days when they could get 'In for a Penny'.

Still, for the residents as for visitors, the Gardens remain the jewel of Kew, and if there will always be some tension between the residents and the administrators—which Joseph Hooker would surely recognise, if not enjoy—it is only because the residents feel a peculiarly personal concern for the Gardens. They have always been *their* gardens.

Appropriately, at the end of the 1980s, there was a reminder too that, long before there were gardens there, Kew was primarily a quay, and a royal quay as well. When the Queen set out to open the new development on Richmond riverside, she went by boat, and embarked—of course—at Cayho.

169 The Princess of Wales Conservatory.

Index

Page numbers in bold type indicate illustrations and maps.

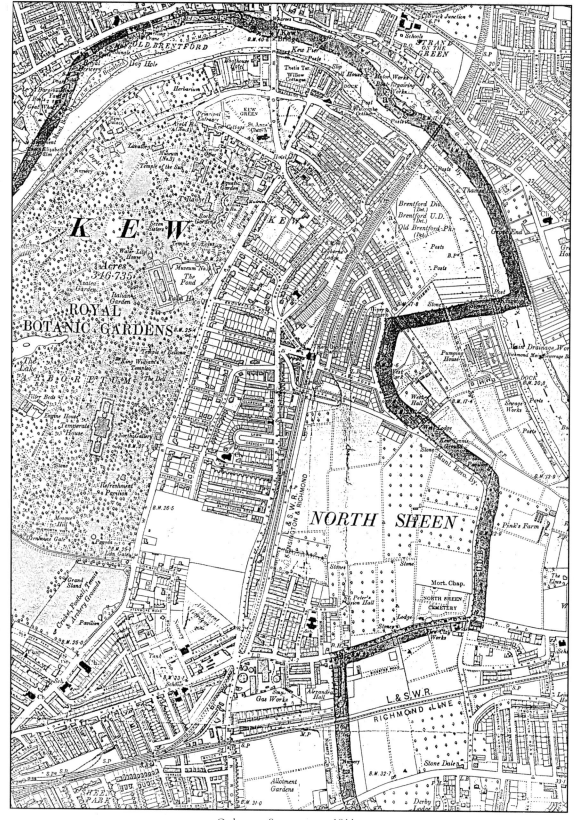

Ordnance Survey map, 1911.